DRUM SET

BY DAVE SCHOEPKE

ISBN: 9798835405640

HOW TO GET THE AUDIO

The audio files for this book are available for free as downloads or streaming on *troynelsonmusic.com*.

We are available to help you with your audio downloads and any other questions you may have. Simply email *help@troynelsonmusic.com*.

See below for the recommended ways to listen to the audio:

Download Audio Files (Zipped)	Stream Audio Files
• Download Audio Files (Zipped)	• Recommended for CELL PHONES & TABLETS
• Recommended for COMPUTERS on WiFi	• Bookmark this page
• A ZIP file will automatically download to the default "downloads" folder on your computer	• Simply tap the PLAY button on the track you want to listen to
• Recommended: download to a desktop/laptop computer *first*, then transfer to a tablet or cell phone	• Files also available for streaming or download at *soundcloud.com/troynelsonbooks*
• Phones & tablets may need an "unzipping" app such as iZip, Unrar or Winzip	
• Download on WiFi for faster download speeds	

> **To download the companion audio files for this book,**
> **visit:** troynelsonmusic.com/audio-downloads/

INTRODUCTION

Hello and welcome to *Drum Set 365!*

The concept behind this book is to provide you, the drummer, with a logical, focused 52-week approach to developing your ability to interpret and perform fundamental rhythms and grooves of over a dozen different styles of drumming. In addition, there are sections that will help you with fills and the development of weakside (left hand and left leg for right-handed drummers) coordination. I have laid this book out in a way that is intended to ease you through the easier styles while working your way up to the more difficult ones, with some exercises interspersed to aid the process.

But why 365 days and why these styles? Well, the styles that I have picked are a cross section of what has permeated popular music the last 60–70 years and exist in many different forms and hybrids across the world. By no means is this book intended to be all-encompassing; instead, the goal is to show you the diversity that exists in music and the different ways the drum set can be approached to assimilate these styles. Hopefully, the book will inspire you to study more in depth the styles that appeal to you the most. In fact, I recommended that you dig past this book for more knowledge, as it's just the tip of the iceberg!

The concept of a daily approach to knowledge is a way to set the bar high enough to achieve your goals. The actuality of attaining and retaining the knowledge daily will be challenging at times because not all of the material can be learned and assimilated that quickly. Nevertheless, don't get discouraged and frustrated by that; instead, try to stay on a continuous path of productivity that works for *you*. In other words, use this book as an organized guide on your path to becoming a better drummer.

To that end, I have chosen drum patterns that are: 1) what many would call "foundation" patterns, ones that are important to style comprehension and appear in many songs within said style, or 2) perhaps not as popular but can be helpful in easing you into requisite coordinations, as some patterns that are "style imperative" can be hard to master without gradual development.

This book is written at the late beginner/early intermediate level and therefore assumes you have a basic understanding of common rhythms and counting systems, as well as knowledge of time signatures and dynamics. If you don't, and you need help, the level of reading comprehension required for this book can be attainted via a general, first-level theory or snare drum method book. Also, this book does not address technique, grips, or stick/pedal manipulations. That material can be attained via various books and online courses. I highly encourage you look into those topics to supplement the material in this book, as they will aid your overall development.

Lastly, developing abilities within any one style is impossible without a serious commitment to listening to music from that style. Therefore, at the end of each week, I have included a list of essential songs to listen to and play along with. As always, be patient with yourself and go slowly. Faster tempos make internalizing rhythms more difficult and actually prolong practice sessions. I've also listed five notable drummers each week. I suggest you research them, watch videos, and listen to recordings they play on. These drummers are benchmark players who have made big impacts on sometimes numerous styles of drumming/music.

The patterns in this book will give you a solid introduction to several musical styles, as well as tools to get you through many different musical situations. However, don't feel like you need to go through this book chronologically; instead, use it in a way that works best for you. But remember: the material becomes more difficult the further you get into the book.

If you have any questions or need assistance with the material, feel free to reach out to me via my website, *daveschoepke.com*. Good luck!

DRUM NOTATION KEY

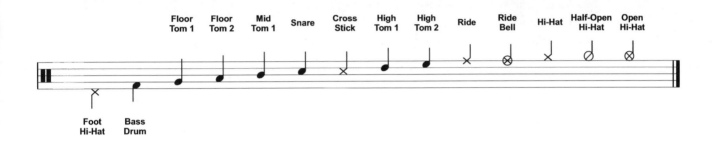

WEEK 1: ROCK 1

The first week of patterns features common rock beats found in countless styles of music. Throughout the week, the bass-drum notes are shifted around a bit while the notes on the ride cymbal, snare, and foot hi-hat remain static. Also, instead of playing steady eighths or quarter notes on the hi-hat, we use our ride cymbal and close the hi-hat with the foot on beats 2 and 4 of each measure. Feel free to lead with whichever hand you are most comfortable (hence, no sticking patterns are included).

MONDAY 1

We start with a two-measure phrase, changing the bass drum in each bar while keeping the other three parts the same throughout.

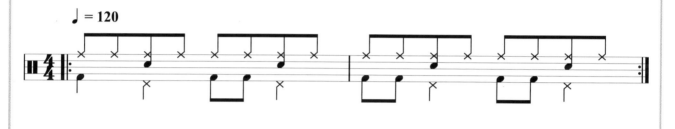

TUESDAY 2

Today, we change the bass drum in each measure, playing on the "and" of beat 3 (bar 1) and beat 1 (bar 2).

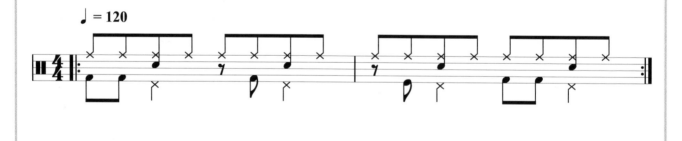

WEDNESDAY

Here, we have more notes on the bass drum but continue to play on the "and" (beat 3 in bar 1, and beat 1 in bar 2).

THURSDAY

Pattern 4 introduces some basic fill ideas, which are notated here for the snare drum. However, I recommend you taking liberty with them and move the 16th notes to different surfaces of your kit. For example, beat 1 on the snare, beats 2 and 3 on the toms, and beat 4 on the floor tom.

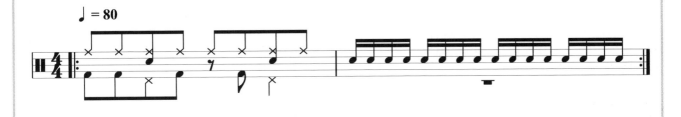

FRIDAY

Pattern 5 introduces the quarter-note ride. Be sure to keep your cymbal pattern steady when you play the bass drum on the "ands," as these patterns are designed to isolate your coordinations a bit and begin to build some independence.

We change up the bass-drum notes further in exercise 6. Be sure to keep everything steady as the notes change.

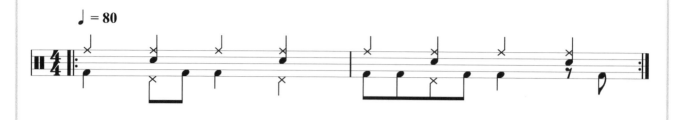

Today features two exercises that use accents. Focus on playing the accented notes (>) louder and the other notes softer, which will help to make the patterns sound cleaner. Also, feel free to move your hands around the kit and strike different surfaces on the accented notes.

SUGGESTED LISTENING AND PLAY-ALONGS:
- "Another One Bites The Dust" Queen
- "Billie Jean" Michael Jackson
- "Pretty Please" Dua Lipa
- "Sgt. Pepper's Lonely Hearts Club Band (Reprise)" The Beatles
- "Springsteen" Eric Church

NOTABLE DRUMMERS:
- Charlie Watts
- Earl Palmer
- Gary Chester
- Hal Blaine
- Ringo Starr

WEEK 2: COUNTRY

This week focuses on traditional country music beats. While newer forms of country utilize many rock-style beat patterns, these grooves are more traditional.

MONDAY 8

Today's exercise focuses on the "train beat," also known as a "country shuffle" or "two-handed shuffle." This groove has two hands on the snare and can be played with sticks, brushes, or multi-rods for a softer effect.

TUESDAY 9

We change the accents for the second pattern. This is a very popular "train beat" used in lots of songs.

WEDNESDAY

Pattern 10 features more shifting accents. It's important to bring out the accented notes, which sometimes use one hand, and sometimes switch from hand to hand. To do this, be sure to quiet down the unaccented notes rather than just hitting the accented notes harder.

THURSDAY

Pattern 11 uses the 6/8 time signature for a slower ballad groove. The snare can also be played as a cross stick for softer dynamics. This groove will resurface in blues and other styles.

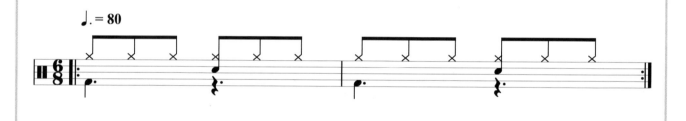

FRIDAY

Another 6/8 beat, this groove adds some 16th notes to the hi-hat on beat 5 of each measure, which gives the groove a bit of a "skipping" feel—a common addition to this type of feel.

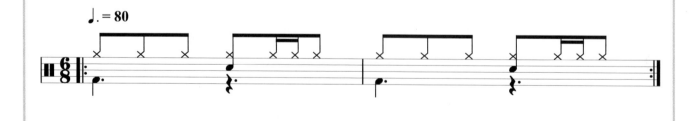

SATURDAY

Pattern 13 is a "train beat" hybrid that mixes up the accents in each measure.

SUNDAY

This pattern is another hybrid that also changes the accents. Remember to quiet down the unaccented notes, which will bring out the groove and make it more dynamic.

SUGGESTED LISTENING AND PLAY-ALONGS:
- "Folsom Prison Blues" Johnny Cash
- "Mammas Don't Let Your Babies Grow Up to Be Cowboys" Waylon Jennings & Willie Nelson
- "On the Road Again" Willie Nelson
- "Crazy" Patsy Cline
- "The Fightin' Side of Me" Merle Haggard

NOTABLE DRUMMERS:
- Larrie Londin
- Eddie Bayers
- W.S. Holland
- Rich Redmond
- Paul Leim

WEEK 3: EDM 1

Week 3 focuses on the first series of EDM beats. This style of drumming is a hybrid of rock, Latin, disco, and funk. There are many offshoots of this style that also combine elements of electronic and programmed drum parts, shifting the role of the drum-set player as the other drum parts take the lead while the acoustic drums support them. It makes for many interesting hybrids.

MONDAY   15

Emphasize the accents on the hi-hats in this groove, which is a general approach to this style, with a very straight feel and a "four on the floor" bass-drum pattern.

TUESDAY   16

Pattern 16 uses open hi-hats on the "ands" in place of the accents, which will come out in an accented way by the nature of the pattern.

WEDNESDAY

Here, we introduce 16th notes on the hi-hat. These beats are often played at fast tempos, so you should play this pattern with both hands in either alternate sticking (R L R L) or one that works for you, as there are many ways to do it to land a hand on the snare for beats 2 and 4.

THURSDAY

Pattern 18 uses accents on the "ands" of each beat in both measures.

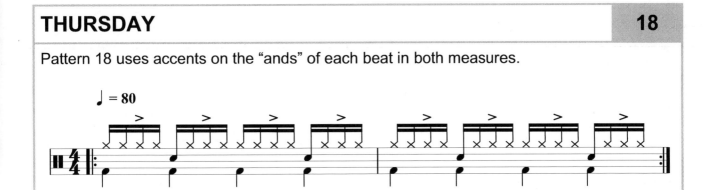

FRIDAY

This pattern swaps out the accented "ands" for opens hi-hats, which makes the beat a little bit trickier.

SATURDAY

Pattern 20 mixes up the snare notes. This is a common move in EDM patterns and can be done many different ways.

SUNDAY

Our seventh day of EDM features two patterns that mix up accents, open hi-hats, and snare notes. These get more creative and can open the door to more hybrids.

SUGGESTED LISTENING AND PLAY-ALONGS:
- "Hey Boy Hey Girl" Chemical Brothers
- "Do the Astral Plane" Flying Lotus
- "BED" Joel Corry, Raye, and David Guetta
- "I Feel Good" Pitbull
- "Get Lucky" Daft Punk

NOTABLE DRUMMERS:
- Michael Schack
- Dennis Bryon
- Tony Thompson
- Earl Young
- Zach Velmer

WEEK 4: ROCK 2

This second week of rock beats features 16th-note combinations on the bass drum and some new snare notes beyond the common "2 and 4" placements. Also, we'll be changing up the ride patterns from eighth notes to quarter notes. Many intricate rock, funk, and new country beats use 16th- and eighth-note combinations on the bass drum and snare, as these patterns show.

MONDAY   22

If you are having trouble putting the notes in the right spots, take the time to count "1-e-&-ah, 2-e-and-ah," etc. for the 16th notes. This will help to make sure that your ride pattern holds steady while you develop this coordination.

♩ = 80

TUESDAY   23

Today's pattern features more combinations of 16th notes and eighth notes on the bass drum.

♩ = 80

WEDNESDAY

Pattern 24 features combinations of eighth notes and 16ths on the bass drum. Keep all of the notes equal in volume so that you develop consistent control and technique.

♩ = 80

THURSDAY

Pattern 25 switches the ride from eighth notes to quarter notes, which may throw you off a bit. But focus on keeping all of the notes steady.

♩ = 80

FRIDAY

Today, we're back to the eighth-note ride pattern and adding the snare on the "and" of beat 4 in both measures.

♩ = 80

SATURDAY

Pattern 27 has us back to the quarter-note ride and introduces snare and bass-drum patterns that change in each measure.

SUNDAY

Our last rock pattern for this week features two two-measure phrases that can be played as one four-measure phrase to test your ability to switch up ride patterns on the fly.

SUGGESTED LISTENING AND PLAY-ALONGS:
- "Sing a Simple Song" Sly & the Family Stone
- "The Immigrant Song" Led Zeppelin
- "Shining Star" Earth, Wind & Fire
- "Vertigo" U2
- "Learn to Fly" Foo Fighters

NOTABLE DRUMMERS:
- John Bonham
- Larry Mullen Jr.
- Dave Grohl
- Phil Rudd
- Roger Hawkins

WEEK 5: EDM 2

This second week on EDM adds some extra moves on the hi-hat and snare to make the patterns a bit more interesting.

MONDAY 29

Pattern 29 adds some new snare drum notes that may be tricky to place at first. So, if you're challenged, then work out the hand patterns first, adding the other parts when you're ready.

TUESDAY 30

Pattern 30 continues the trend of adding snare notes, this time to the "ah" of some beats. These notes are mixed with notes that you're already familiar with.

WEDNESDAY

This pattern opens the hi-hat consistently on the "and" of each beat. This is a very common pattern that originated in disco but has been use in many other grooves/styles, as well. Getting to the snare from the hi-hat in time is tricky, so pace yourself with this coordination.

THURSDAY

Here, we open the hi-hat on the "and" of every beat except beat 2. This subtle change might be problematic at first, so take it slow.

FRIDAY

Pattern 33 combines new snare note placements with open hi-hats, which make this beat a bit different. After you lock it down, try your own combinations.

SATURDAY

A common EDM beat, Pattern 34 differs from Pattern 33 by one (fewer) snare drum note.

SUNDAY

The last pattern of the week uses all of the previous options, plus 16th-note hi-hat patterns.

SUGGESTED LISTENING AND PLAY-ALONGS:
- "Disco Inferno" The Trammps
- "Night Fever" Bee Gees
- "Heartbreak Anthem" Galantis, David Guetta & Little Mix
- "Le Freak" Chic
- "Flood" Nerve

NOTABLE DRUMMERS:
- Adam Deitch
- Jojo Mayer
- Ash Soan
- Dan Snaith
- KJ Sawka

WEEK 6: BLUES 1

This week, we start working on blues and shuffle patterns. The shuffle is a main ingredient in the blues style and is also used in rock, jazz, country, funk, and many other genres, with minor or dramatic embellishments added to fit the dynamics. Take your time with the shuffle, as it can be deceptively difficult to play, especially at faster tempos. The blues is a deep style that really requires some in-depth listening to master the subtle details that enhance the groove.

MONDAY   36

Pattern 36 is a slow blues groove written in 4/4 but you will see it in 6/8 and 12/8, as well.

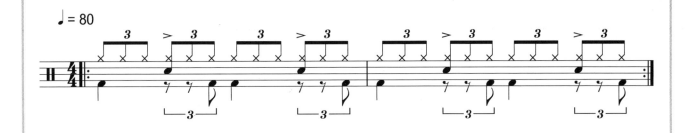

TUESDAY   37

Pattern 37 is another slow blues groove but with additional bass drum notes to create a more driving feel that can make the pattern feel heavier.

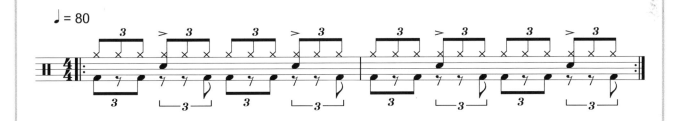

WEDNESDAY

This pattern can be played as a slow blues groove or as a faster shuffle feel.

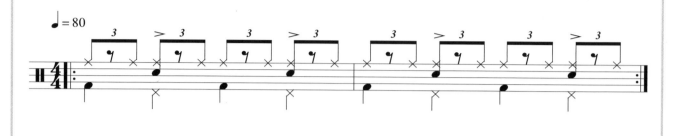

THURSDAY

This "Flat Tire" groove is a common blues pattern that has a back-and-forth feel, kind of like a hiccup.

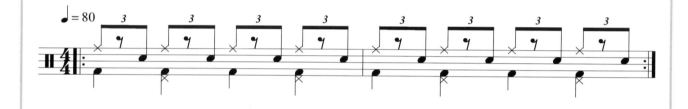

FRIDAY

The first of many shuffles to come, this pattern is a basic shuffle that can be used for many styles, depending on your dynamics. If you've never played a shuffle, this one can be difficult at first, so work up your snare hand gradually.

SATURDAY

This is a slow blues variation similar to Pattern 37 but with the bass drum broken up a bit more, giving the groove some more space.

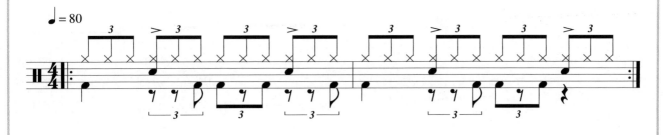

SUNDAY

Here's a shuffle with a two-handed buildup that is common in many song forms. Don't force it; instead, work on building it slowly. You can play either—or both—of the buildup notes on any two surfaces of the kit, so experiment with different combinations.

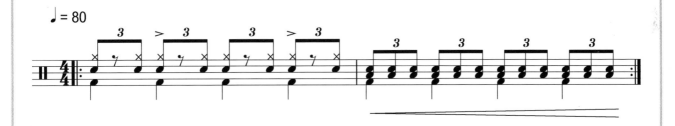

SUGGESTED LISTENING AND PLAY-ALONGS:
- "The Letter" B.B. King
- "Boom Boom" John Lee Hooker
- "Spoonful" Willie Dixon
- "Manish Boy" Muddy Waters
- "Moanin' at Midnight" Howlin' Wolf

NOTABLE DRUMMERS:
- Sam Lay
- Willie Smith
- Steve Jordan
- Fred Below
- Jabo Starks

WEEK 7: LINEAR FILLS 1

Week 7 gets us into *linear fills*, which are patterns that can be played many different ways and have multiple sticking options that you can try. Linear fills can also be played as grooves for songs by repeating pieces of the pattern. The main thing about linear fills and beat patterns is that there are few—and sometimes just one—note being played at a time (there are many exceptions, though), which creates a very funky, almost disjointed sound that can add a really fun flair to your drumming style. Start by playing these patterns with sticking combinations that are comfortable for you and then challenge yourself to expand the way you think about the instrument. Patterns like these can really open up your playing.

MONDAY   43

The first pattern is a typical approach to linear drumming. There are two notes on the snare and one apiece on the hi-hat and bass drum. You can approach this with any sticking combination you like.

TUESDAY   44

This pattern starts with the bass drum and then puts the middle two notes on the hi-hat, which can be a challenge, balance-wise, because a softer part of the kit is in the middle of a note sequence. Nonetheless, keep all of the notes clear and even.

WEDNESDAY

Pattern 45 switches the bass and snare notes around. If you try a sticking pattern in which back-to-back notes are played with one hand, you will open up some new directions and coordinations.

THURSDAY

Taking the 16th notes and creating a sequence in which you play three notes in a row, each on a different surface, makes it feel like you're playing in 3/4 time. Breaking up the notes in creative ways can be a really interesting way to play.

FRIDAY

Here, we continue to break up the 16th notes, which will be more interesting if you experiment with the sticking.

Pattern 48 is specifically designed to be played with one hand on the hi-hat and the other on the snare (although you certainly can change it up). Keeping your hands in place will alternate which hand is the lead hand, which is a good skill to develop.

Pattern 49 is a four-measure phrase that mixes in all of the ideas from this week. Some elements of this pattern may come across as beat patterns on their own. If you find some of that in here, feel free to take those ideas and experiment with them.

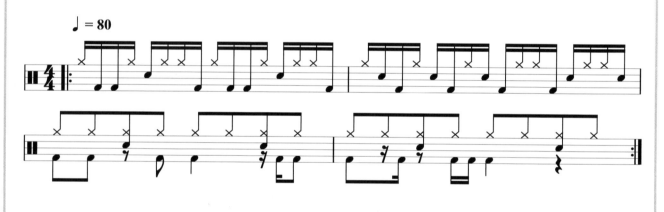

SUGGESTED LISTENING AND PLAY-ALONGS:
- "Motor Booty Affair" Parliament
- "Cissy Strut" The Meters
- "50 Ways to Leave Your Lover" Paul Simon
- "Satisfaction" Devo
- "U.S. Drag" Missing Persons

NOTABLE DRUMMERS:
- Zigaboo Modeliste
- Steve Gadd
- Terry Bozzio
- Dennis Chambers
- David Garibaldi

WEEK 8: ROCK 3

Week 8 features rock patterns with increasing difficulty on the kick drum and more fill ideas incorporating the bass drum.

MONDAY   50

Here, we start to use more 16th-note combinations on the bass drum. This pattern gets deeper into groups of three notes on the kick. Play them evenly and don't rush.

♩ = 80

TUESDAY   51

Pattern 51 continues the three-note combos on the kick, including going across the bar line of the two-measure phrase.

♩ = 80

WEDNESDAY

Look out for the transition between measure 1 and measure 2, where there are quite a few notes to deal with. Again, keep the notes clean and even and try to put as much space between them as possible.

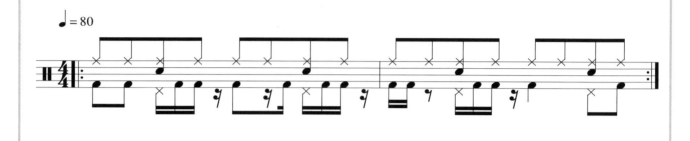

THURSDAY

Pattern 53 has some subtle changes. You may have noticed some beats are considerably easier for you than others, while some, particularly earlier in your study, were more difficult. This is due to the increased development and evolution of your coordinations and limb independence.

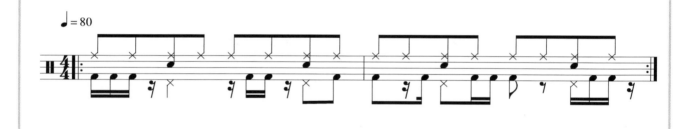

FRIDAY

Sometimes, you'll find it very challenging to play note groupings placed in certain spots in the measure. That's often due to playing notes in spots that are relatively new to you. Look at that as a positive and part of identifying your weaknesses.

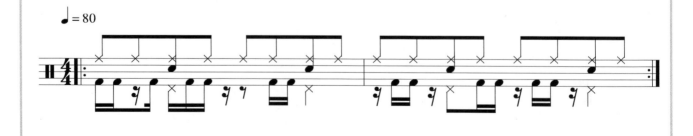

SATURDAY

Today, we head back to linear-based fill ideas. This pattern is very common and can be used both as a fill and as an exercise to build up control and speed while playing two notes with one foot. Make sure all of the notes are even and sound like a cohesive group of 4 rather than two sets of 2.

SUNDAY

Pattern 56 moves the bass drum notes to the "e" and the "and" (beat 4, bar 1), which may feel awkward at first. Once you get the sequence sorted out, you will discover that there are many ways to play it. Like all of the fills in this book, experimenting with moving your hands to different surfaces once you get comfortable is a good idea. It expands the fills exponentially and challenges you to balance your limbs to even out the sounds.

SUGGESTED LISTENING AND PLAY-ALONGS:
- "Open My Eyes" Rival Sons
- "It's Your Thing" Isley Brothers
- "Signed, Sealed, Delivered" Stevie Wonder
- "Dani California" Red Hot Chili Peppers
- "Talking to Myself" Linkin Park

NOTABLE DRUMMERS:
- Ian Paice
- Richie Hayward
- Omar Hakim
- Hannah Ford-Welton
- Keith Moon

WEEK 9: BOSSA NOVA 1

This week, we introduce our first Latin rhythms, the Bossa Nova from Brazil. For the most part, Latin styles originate on percussion and have been adapted to drum set through the years. Because of this, the coordination is more challenging and may take some time to get together.

MONDAY

Take your time sorting through this first pattern, ensuring that you can maintain a consistent bass drum pattern. When you have that together, add the hands.

TUESDAY

We shift the cross-stick notes on this one. Make sure you're locked in on the bass drum notes before you add the cross stick by doing some reps of just the bass drum and hi-hat.

WEDNESDAY

Pattern 59 features another shift in the cross stick. Be sure to hold the stick loosely, getting the thick part of the stick to make solid contact with the rim while keeping the opposite end on the drum. Players will often lay the stick horizontally across the drum and/or flip the stick so the butt end is hitting the rim. Either way, the fullest sound is achieved when the thicker part of the stick is on the rim.

THURSDAY

Latin styles, in general, use a softer touch on the bass drum, so try to play it with about 50% less volume than what you use for rock. A softer bass drum will help the other sounds of the kit come out and result in a lighter sound overall, which is what the style requires to blend with the other instruments.

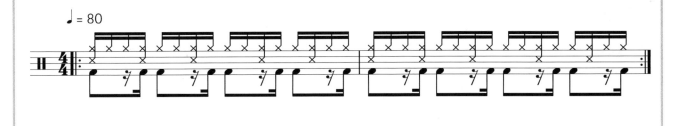

FRIDAY

Another shift in cross-stick notes, Pattern 61 is a 2-3 son clave pattern, which you'll be seeing more of when we get to Afro-Cuban patterns. It may take some time to get this pattern locked in, so be patient with yourself.

Pattern 62 uses the Partido Alto pattern for the cross stick. This is a Brazilian rhythm often used in Bossa Nova and Samba, as well as other Latin styles. Oftentimes, the whole ensemble will follow and accentuate this rhythmic pattern, but that is just an option.

Pattern 63 uses some hi-hat opens to add some spice to the groove. These rhythms can be played with brushes, rods, or even hands to assimilate a variety of dynamics.

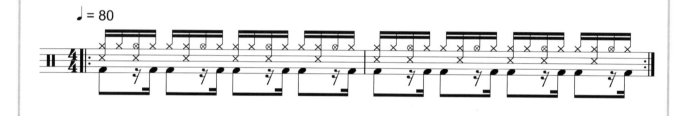

SUGGESTED LISTENING AND PLAY-ALONGS:
- "Desafinado" Milton Banana
- "Corcovado" Antonio Carlos Jobim
- "Agua De Beber" Quarteto Jobim
- "Rio" Quarteto do Rio
- "Este Seu Olhar" Nara Leão

NOTABLE DRUMMERS:
- Buddy Deppenschmidt
- Edison Machado
- Milton Banana
- Duduka Da Fonseca
- Dom Um Romão

WEEK 10: BOSSA NOVA 2

We continue this week with more Bossa Nova and a few changes, including switching to the ride cymbal and adding hi-hat closes with the foot on the "and" of every beat. This is a common way to phrase the Bossa and prepares us for the Samba patterns later in the book. While there are certainly other ways to play the hi-hat with the foot, this is a very common approach. Take your time making sure you can get both feet coordinated and then add your hands when you have them locked in.

MONDAY · 64

This first groove uses a familiar cross-stick pattern from the first week of Bossa Nova. The added hi-hat with your foot will be a new challenge, so be patient.

TUESDAY · 65

Watch for the hi-hat foot wanting to follow the cross stick pattern, which is a common issue. Also, do reps on the feet before adding the new cross-stick notes.

WEDNESDAY

Remember to "feather" the bass drum notes, playing them soft enough to be heard underneath the cross-stick notes, which will enhance the groove and fit with the style much better in a traditional situation.

THURSDAY

If you're having a hard time controlling the bass drum volume at first, don't obsess over it. Once you get control of the coordinations, you can work on the dynamics and gradually quiet the bass drum down.

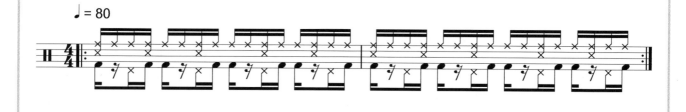

FRIDAY

Here, we have the Afro-Cuban 2-3 son clave again, which could be played in reverse, as well. We could employ other Afro-Cuban clave patterns within this style, too.

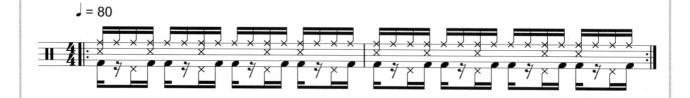

This is a common pattern that you will frequently see in Brazilian styles of music.

The Partido Alto pattern returns. By now, you should have quite a few options for the Bossa Nova, but we can also alter the hi-hat and bass drum notes, as well as change the tone of the drums by using mallets, different types of sticks, brushes, or our hands. There are many books that go into greater detail on Brazilian rhythms.

SUGGESTED LISTENING AND PLAY-ALONGS:
- "Vivo Sonhando" Sérgio Mendes
- "Soul Sauce" Cal Tjader
- "Blue Bossa" Joe Henderson
- "Come to the Mardi Gras" Tito Puente
- "Triste" Elis Regina & Antonio Carlos Jobim

NOTABLE DRUMMERS:
- Bobby Sanabria
- Airto Moreira
- Tito Puente
- Willie Bobo
- Rudy Collins

WEEK 11: ROCK 4

This week, we get into some new eighth- and 16th-note hi-hat patterns, which will give your grooves a funkier edge and prep you for some of the challenges in funk, Afrobeat, and other Latin styles.

MONDAY   71

Note that the hi-hat pattern is three unbroken notes in a row. This may be tricky to play at first, so ease into it and don't push the tempo.

TUESDAY   72

Note that this hi-hat pattern has a break on the "e" but will feel like the previous pattern at times if you are not counting steadily. So, make sure that you are or you will just slip back into Pattern 71.

WEDNESDAY

Offbeat notes (notes on the "and") may feel odd to you because you are so used to playing more notes, but notice what happens to the groove when you add space (rests)—the hi-hat almost acts like a percussion instrument rather than part of the drum set.

THURSDAY

If you're struggling with the new coordinations, then simplify the bass and snare patterns to just a quarter note each (bass on beats 1 and 3 and snare on beats 2 and 4), which will help you to focus on keeping your new hi-hat patterns steady and accurate.

FRIDAY

Be sure to count your way through every measure to ensure your accuracy and keep you from learning the pattern the wrong way.

SATURDAY

This pattern adds more notes to the bass drum but you can also add more notes to the hi-hat, as well as some accents and opens—things you will discover in the funk and Afrobeat styles coming up later in the book.

SUNDAY

This week's final pattern is a hybrid of two hi-hat patterns within a two-measure phrase. This approach can be applied many ways, including within the same measure. Whatever works with the music you are playing is always what matters most. These patterns are merely a starting point on your quest to finding more ways to be creative.

SUGGESTED LISTENING AND PLAY-ALONGS:
- "Life Itself" Glass Animals
- "Empty Pages" Traffic
- "Bell Bottom Blues" Derek & the Dominos
- "I Can't Give Everything Away" David Bowie
- "The Ghost of You" My Chemical Romance

NOTABLE DRUMMERS:
- Kenny Aronoff
- Jim Gordon
- Josh Freese
- Jeff Porcaro
- Travis Barker

WEEK 12: ROCK OSTINATOS

We take a bit of a break this week from beats to work on some independence in your hi-hat and bass drum. These patterns are rock-based and focus on maintaining steady foot patterns while working different combinations with your hands over the top.

MONDAY

This first pattern uses doubles in each hand against the bass drum on the beat and the hi-hat on the "ands." This type of exercise is good for working different sticking options against your foot patterns.

♩ = 80

TUESDAY

Here, Pattern 78 is reversed, which will be good for working your weak hand in leading the note sequence. This alone can really open up your approach options around the kit.

♩ = 80

WEDNESDAY

Pattern 80 simply uses alternating singles and then switches to doubles within the measure. The reason for this is to open up more possibilities and to aid in mobility around the kit if you choose to move to different surfaces.

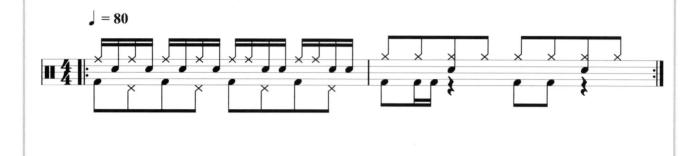

THURSDAY

Here, we invert the doubles, which gives us some new sounds and, if you move these around the kit, will open up new fill ideas and directions.

FRIDAY

This is the reversal of Pattern 81 and, again, will flip your leading hands around if you haven't already. In doing so, you will build more dexterity and independence, which, in turn, gives you many more sound choices. Some of this material will lend itself to opening up new ways to solo over the top of what you are doing with your feet.

SATURDAY

The *paradiddle*, a specific series of single strokes and double strokes, finally arrives in this book (and you will see it again in other sections). The paradiddle is a great pattern for checking your hand/foot coordination because it forces you to flip to the other side to lead. If you are new to this great rudiment, take your time and work slowly. The reward for getting comfortable with this pattern is plentiful.

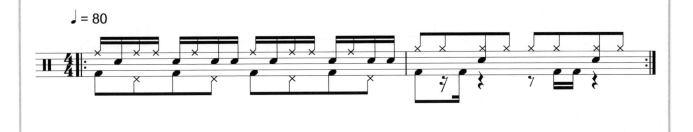

SUNDAY

This week's final pattern is a mixed-sticking combination that uses one side of the paradiddle. This is a small sample of all the different ways you can work your hand coordination against whatever you do with your feet. *Stick Control* and *Master Studies* are two books that have a large variety of sticking combinations that you can superimpose.

SUGGESTED LISTENING AND PLAY-ALONGS:
- "Gypsy Eyes" Jimi Hendrix
- "Where the Streets Have No Name" U2
- "How to Fight Loneliness" Wilco
- "War Pigs" Black Sabbath
- "Gold Dust" Fleetwood Mac

NOTABLE DRUMMERS:
- Mick Fleetwood
- Mitch Mitchell
- Glenn Kotche
- Buddy Rich
- Jon Fishman

WEEK 13: REVIEW 1

Congratulations! You made it to the first review. This week is all about looking at the material you've worked on this far and making sure that you're keeping it close at hand so you can apply it comfortably to some degree. These patterns are a cross section of what you have gone through but there is certainly more to review if you have the time. The suggested tempos are closer to the tempos you would hear and play them at in a musical situation.

MONDAY   85

This first pattern is the country "train beat." Be sure to bring out your accents by quieting down the other notes, which is always a good way to make your accents stand out.

TUESDAY   86

EDM is represented next. We have some hi-hat opens to go along with 16ths and steady quarter notes on the bass drum to anchor the pattern.

WEDNESDAY

Pattern 87 is the blues shuffle. If you haven't revisited this at all, then pay attention to the accents on beats 2 and 4 of each measure. Again, keeping the other notes down will really bring out the accents and make this feel groove nicely.

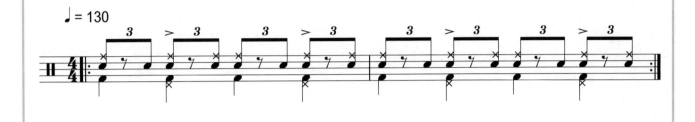

THURSDAY

Here, we have some fill work with a rock beat. If you're comfortable with this pattern, then spend some time moving your hands around the kit freely, experimenting with different sound combinations.

FRIDAY

For the Bossa Nova review pattern, we revisit the Partido Alto. This is a note sequence that you will often see in Brazilian music, so getting comfortable with it now will help you greatly.

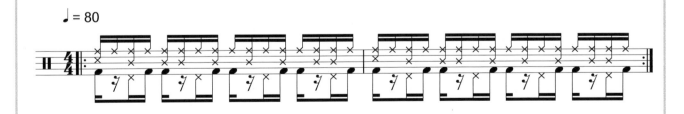

SATURDAY

Pattern 90 uses some three-note hi-hat patterns. Reviewing this pattern now will prepare you for the funk, Afrobeat, Samba, and Baião styles coming later in this book.

SUNDAY

Ostinato study wraps up our first review, which should help prepare you for some of the upcoming work in this book. There are many complex patterns in the styles ahead that use mixed sticking like this, so you won't be a stranger to that approach when you get to it.

WEEK 14: SWING

This week, we start working on *swing*, which is one of the first manifestations of early jazz. There are a couple of things that are important for capturing the dynamics of the style. First, work on "feathering" the bass drum, which is the practice of playing the bass drum very soft within the groove. Think of the bass drum as a texture rather than a main volume component like in rock styles. This can be challenging when first starting this style. Second, the ride pattern and hi-hat are important for the feel to come across in a relaxed "swinging" manner. It is really important to listen to the audio examples and others to understand what that sound is and how to approach playing the set.

MONDAY 92

Pattern 92 is a typical swing pattern with a cross stick on beat 4 of each measure. This is a good pattern to start with to help you work towards the dynamic balance of this style.

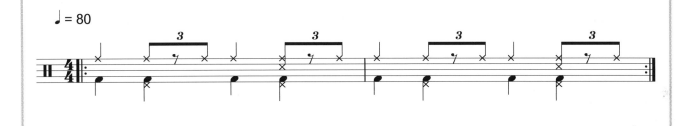

TUESDAY 93

From here through the rest of the patterns, we go to the snare and begin to work on independence. The snare drum volume and dexterity need to be controlled and relative to the sound of the rest of the kit. This note combination works as a groove pattern for a "shout" chorus and, in that context, could be played louder to approximate the dynamics of the band.

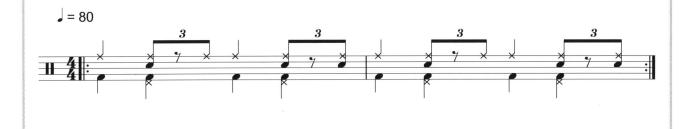

A swing/big band group is a very dynamic and exciting musical scenario. To work within this music, you need to have a high level of control over the independence of your snare drum because it acts a dynamic complement to the music. All of the drum kit operates in this manner, of course, but the snare is the component that can shift and shape the music the most. This pattern starts to work new note positions into the swing groove.

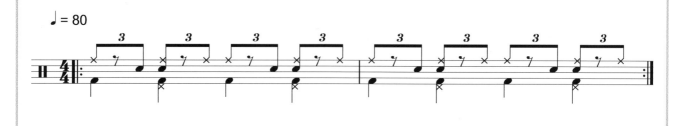

This pattern adds some new notes, beginning on beat 1 of each measure, which may take a bit to sort out, balance-wise.

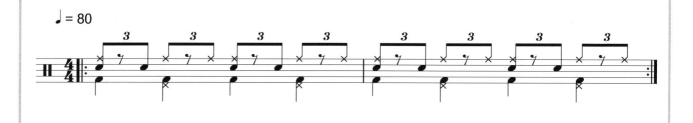

Here, notes appear in different places across the measure. Try to work on playing them at many different dynamic levels. You can also apply accents if you feel that you have the control to do so.

SATURDAY

Pattern 97 will give you more of an "off-beat" feel and, again, puts some notes in new places. Begin to push the tempo when you feel comfortable and have some dynamic control.

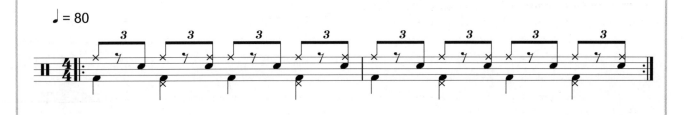

SUNDAY

The last groove of the week mixes up two measures and adds some new challenges. One thing you can do with all of the content this week is play pattern 1 (bar 1) for two measures and then play the exercise as written to give you a four-measure phrase. You will hear these concepts in the music that you can study from the list provided. Listen to the high level of dynamic control of this music and the mastery over the instrument that is required to play this music at a high level.

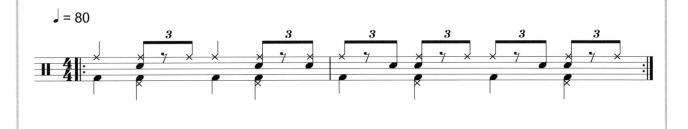

SUGGESTED LISTENING AND PLAY-ALONGS:
- "It Don't Mean a Thing (If It Ain't Got That Swing)" Duke Ellington and Ella Fitzgerald
- "Dream a Little Dream of Me" Ella Fitzgerald and Louis Armstrong
- "Fly Me to the Moon" Frank Sinatra and Count Basie
- "So What" Miles Davis
- "Moanin'" Art Blakey and the Jazz Messengers

NOTABLE DRUMMERS:
- Chick Webb
- Jo Jones
- Gene Krupa
- Viola Smith
- Jimmy Cobb

WEEK 15: METAL 1

Week 15 brings us to some concepts in metal drumming and its offshoots, of which there are many. Thrash, Death, Speed, Grindcore, Black Metal, Nu-metal, and so many more. A key point of these styles is the extensive use of double bass. Although there are no rules, it supports the rhythmic intensity of the music and punctuates the complex bass and guitar parts, with many elements played in unison for maximum effect. So, if you don't play double bass, then move past the metal sections, as they all feature extensive double-bass patterns throughout. If you are new to double bass, however, there are patterns here to get you going—just be sure to stay relaxed, consistent, and note how your patterns are sounding and if there is a solid balance before you push into faster tempos.

MONDAY   99

Pattern 99 is a stock 16th-note pattern that is a prerequisite to functioning on double bass within this style. I suggest you play this as alternating notes but you can certainly devise a sequence that works best for you.

TUESDAY   100

We begin to break the notes up into groups of 3, which can certainly be done with one foot at slower tempos but is harder at really fast ones. The ability to stop and start at will is important and this begins to work on that.

WEDNESDAY

Alternating longer and shorter note sequences comes next. Here, you can certainly get creative with organizing the notes, although I suggest doing alternating singles first, and then experimenting.

THURSDAY

Here, we begin to break up the notes in familiar ways. You can try mixing up approaches for more control; for example: RL LRL LRL RRL L.

FRIDAY

Pattern 103 features seven-note groupings that travel across the beat and, when played for two measures or more, across the bar line, as well.

Pattern 104 gives us some off-beat combos that can break up your leading foot in interesting ways. Practice switching up which foot restarts the phrase, which will give you more dexterity.

The last pattern for this week mixes up the notes over two measures. I suggest practicing these patterns in different back-to-back combinations, which will give you a pretty good start on the basics of double bass. You cannot force this type of control; you need to be patient while working up your feet to play with as much balance as possible. Concentrate on the sound of the notes, making sure everything is clean and concise.

SUGGESTED LISTENING AND PLAY-ALONGS:
- "Lightning Strike" Judas Priest
- "Battery" Metallica
- "A Light in the Black" Rainbow
- "Ace of Spades" Motörhead
- "Detox" Strapping Young Lad

NOTABLE DRUMMERS:
- Nicko McBrain
- Bill Ward
- Mike Portnoy
- Carmine Appice
- Charlie Benante

WEEK 16: ROCK 5

Our last week on rock takes us into more challenging coordinations between the snare and bass drum while keeping eighth notes going on the hi-hat or ride—whichever you choose. These patterns will be helpful for when funk, Afrobeat, jazz, and Latin styles show up in the weeks ahead. Those other styles will require "ghost" notes, which will be challenging, so getting familiar with this bit of independence will be helpful.

MONDAY — 106

The first pattern this week begins by placing a snare note on the "e" of beats 1 and 3. You may struggle with keeping your leading hand steady, so, if you need to, play the pattern without the bass drum, and then add that later.

TUESDAY — 107

Moving the snare to the "ah" of beats 2 and 4 here will require you to face challenges similar to ones you faced in Pattern 106. The same approach should work; just don't force it.

WEDNESDAY 108

Pattern 108 ups the note content, which almost makes the groove feel like it's played in double-time. Once you get the coordination together, move to your ride and take your snare hand around the kit, hitting whatever sounds you have available. This will open up the pattern considerably and make it feel like a fill and a groove at the same time.

THURSDAY 109

Take the same approach here as you did yesterday, moving your snare hand around the kit. Also, you can split the notes between different surfaces, which will help build up your dexterity and add another challenge.

FRIDAY 110

Here, we move the two snare notes to the middle of the beat, which will make the pattern feel a bit different than the previous two. Be sure to keep everything sounding even and clean.

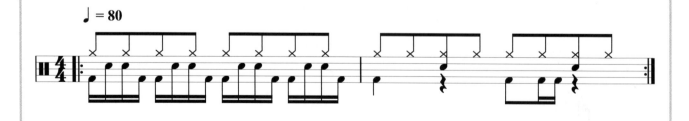

Pattern 111 reverses the sequence and may be even trickier than the last one but, when played evenly, should sound pretty nice and also prep you for some of the Latin material coming soon.

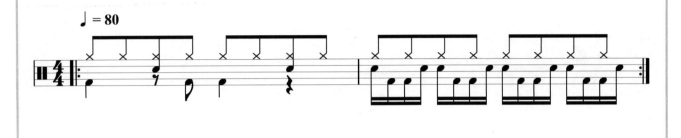

The final groove of the week mixes up some of this week's ideas and, as a whole, can be played as a two-measure groove with notes moving around the kit, or as a beat with a one-measure fill that also moves around. Experiment with the options, and you will get a lot more out of the material.

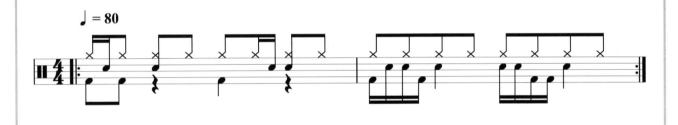

SUGGESTED LISTENING AND PLAY-ALONGS:
- "Weird Fishes" Radiohead
- "Criminal" Fiona Apple
- "Rock Your Body" Justin Timberlake
- "Change (In the House of Flies)" Deftones
- "You Can't Always Get What You Want" Rolling Stones

NOTABLE DRUMMERS:
- Steve Smith
- Steve Ferrone
- Gregg Bissonette
- Cindy Blackman
- Levon Helm

WEEK 17: FUNK 1

Week 17 takes us to funk. Here is where we start to focus on more subtle details such as ghost notes, accents, and varying hi-hat patterns. This style is firmly rooted in a rock-steady groove that relies less on fills and more on subtle elements that propel the songs. Sometimes minimal changes within a song are what make a big difference in the dynamics.

Be sure to focus on creating contrasts within your dynamics so that they're heard in full effect. In regard to capturing those details, take each element one layer at a time, adding new pieces when you feel comfortable rather than trying to put it all together at once. As always, go slow and be patient.

MONDAY   113

The first groove uses ghost notes on the "e" and "ah" of some of the beats and also incorporates accents on beats 2 and 4 of each measure. Try to play the ghost notes as soft as possible while playing the accented notes nice and strong.

TUESDAY   114

Pattern 114 gets a little bit more involved—for example, it changes the bass drum notes and varies the ghost notes—so add the bass drum only after you get your hands locked in.

WEDNESDAY

Here, we change the hi-hat part to the familiar three 16ths. With the inclusion of ghost notes, it may take some time to sort the coordination. In other words, you may need to run those notes a bit before you add the other elements.

THURSDAY

Now that we are confident with the changed hi-hat pattern, some trickier bass drum and snare notes add some difficulty to this pattern.

FRIDAY

Today, we change the hi-hat pattern again, this time to another familiar sequence. Despite the familiarity, getting comfortable with the new pattern will take some time. This is an example of why it's really important to count every beat; otherwise, you may slip back to the pattern you played on the previous two days.

Here, we use the hi-hat pattern from yesterday but the added complexity in the bass drum and ghost notes make things trickier.

The last pattern of the week brings us back to playing the offbeat on the hi-hat, which, after playing so many notes for a few days, feels like big gaps between your strikes. Again, counting consistently will really help you sort out the pattern.

SUGGESTED LISTENING AND PLAY-ALONGS:
- "Talkin' Loud and Sayin' Nothing" James Brown
- "Shining Star" Earth, Wind & Fire
- "Skate" Silk Sonic
- "Kiss" Prince
- "The Fire" The Roots

NOTABLE DRUMMERS:
- Clyde Stubblefield
- Melvin Parker
- Questlove
- Benny Benjamin
- James Gadson

WEEK 18: AFROBEAT 1

Afrobeat is a very unique style of music and drumming. It has been a relatively underground style of music but, in the last 25 years, has grown in popularity. The coordinations for Afrobeat are tricky and unique to this style yet have some similarities to funk, rock, jazz, and Latin. Like funk, this style of drumming relies heavily on repetition but can have more subtle variations like in jazz. There are some placements of bass drum notes that are different from what you may have seen and a lot of times the beat may feel "turned around," with notes in uncommon spots. Review the recommended listening to orient yourself with what is happening in the music, as there can be many instruments moving in and out of parts of songs and lots of percussion (sometimes an Afrobeat ensemble can have 20 or more players).

Lastly, you will see that the notation includes hand hi-hat, as well as opens and closes with the foot. This is a big part of the style but it's tricky. The sound may change each time you open the hi-hat but try to open it just a little bit so you can hear the cymbals close a little within each pattern.

MONDAY | 120

This first Afrobeat pattern uses a familiar three-note pattern on the hi-hat but with some different placements of the snare drum. The subtle closing of the foot hi-hat while you are also playing it with the hand will be the biggest challenge, though. If you have to open it a lot at first, that's fine. But then gradually close it to a subtle open.

♩ = 80

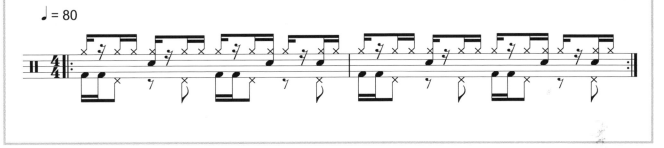

TUESDAY | 121

The snare and bass drum are inverted from their common spot in backbeat-oriented music for this beat, so that may take you a bit to get comfortable with. When you do get comfortable, however, it will be an asset to the way you interpret and phrase a groove.

♩ = 80

WEDNESDAY

The third Afrobeat pattern simplifies some of the bass drum notes to give us a slightly different flavor while maintaining the basic approach.

THURSDAY

There isn't one snare hit in a "normal" spot in this groove but this is part of what makes Afrobeat drumming unique. This type of groove is a very common approach but isn't always easy to assimilate.

FRIDAY

Pattern 124 is *the* must-know Afrobeat groove, according to innovator Tony Allen, but it isn't an easy one. Go slow and make sure you can capture all the notes.

We invert the snare and bass for Pattern 125 and add some more notes on the snare. By now, you should be getting comfortable with this fun style of music. Note that the hi-hat has shifted to just eighth notes for this one.

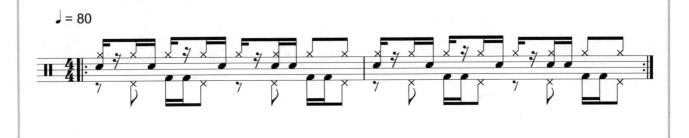

Pattern 126 maintains the inverted bass and snare but with some additional complexity. The eighth notes on the hi-hat are carried over from the previous pattern, however.

SUGGESTED LISTENING AND PLAY-ALONGS:
- "Gentleman" Fela Kuti
- "Go Back" Tony Allen
- "Beng Beng Beng" Femi Kuti
- "Si, Se Puede" Antibalas
- "Upside Down" Fela Kuti & the Africa 70

NOTABLE DRUMMERS:
- Tony Allen
- Fela Kuti
- Ginger Baker
- Kevin Raczka
- Cheikh Lo

WEEK 19: SWING/BOP OSTINATOS

This is the second week of ostinato exercises, but this time we move into the swing/bop style. We are applying the common four-bass-notes-to-the-bar pattern, with foot hi-hat on beats 2 and 4, both of which are hallmark ostinato patterns in this style.

When playing songs in the swing/bop style, the bass drum is played softly (feathered); therefore, after you get comfortable with the coordinations, practice playing the bass as soft as you can to work on your dynamic control. These patterns will help prep you for the upcoming bebop material.

MONDAY   127

Our first swing/bop pattern goes to straight, alternate-sticked triplets on the snare in measure 2. You can experiment with this pattern in a couple of ways: start by moving your hands around the kit to all of your surfaces, then try different sticking combinations.

TUESDAY   128

Pattern 128 incorporates the ride cymbal into the triplets, which, by design, means that the first note of each triplet is played with the same hand. But, if your ride is in an accessible spot, you may be able to play it with alternate sticking. Choose whichever methods works best for you.

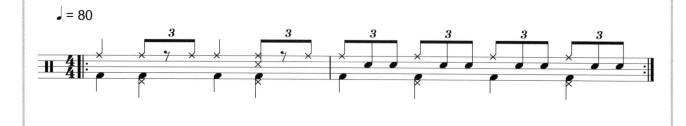

WEDNESDAY

The ride/hi-hat pattern here is inverted from the one in Pattern 128 but you can approach it the same way.

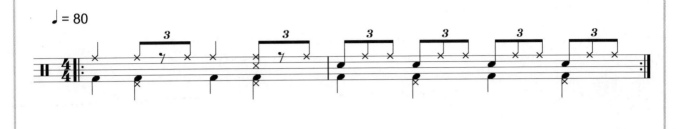

THURSDAY

We incorporate the double-stroke roll for this exercise, which makes for interesting phrasing of the triplets, as we're doing sort of a "two-in-three" sequence. This is very common in various forms of jazz and other music and can be applied to any part of the kit between the feet and hands.

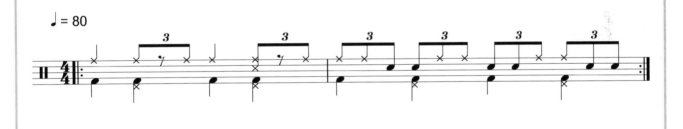

FRIDAY

Pattern 131 mixes up alternate strokes with doubles, which leads us into paradiddle territory.

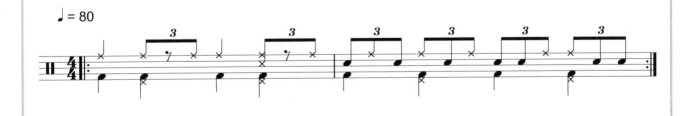

SATURDAY

This pattern is the flipped version of yesterday's pattern. Sometimes when you flip the direction of a sequence of notes, new challenges arise and weaknesses in your ability to phrase notes in different parts of the measure are revealed. Hence, why it's important to do these things.

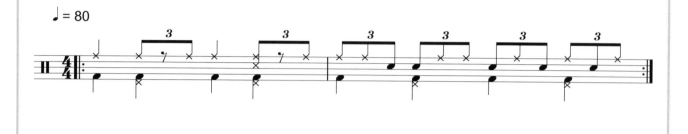

SUNDAY

Pattern 133 continues the practice of mixing up singles and doubles, again implying paradiddle ideas.

SUGGESTED LISTENING AND PLAY-ALONGS:
- "Freedom Jazz Dance" Miles Davis
- "Mercy, Mercy, Mercy" Cannonball Adderley
- "The Groove Merchant" Thad Jones & Mel Lewis
- "The Anxious Battle for Sanity" Antonio Sanchez
- "Midnight Special" Jimmy Smith

NOTABLE DRUMMERS:
- Mel Lewis
- Sonny Payne
- Dannie Richmond
- Ed Thigpen
- Terri Lyne Carrington

WEEK 20: SAMBA 1

The Samba, a close relative of the Bossa Nova, is our next step into Brazilian music. You will recognize the ostinatos played with your feet but the challenges here will be in building your independence on the snare with more activity and varied note choices (as well as multiple ride patterns, which we will explore in coming weeks). Make sure you are solid with the ostinatos before you tackle the patterns.

All of these patterns are written for the snare drum but you can play them as cross-stick patterns, too. So, if you have time, work those in, as well. Lastly, keep in mind that Samba and most Latin styles originated on percussion and, over time, were adapted to drum set.

MONDAY   134

Our first Samba pattern brings us eighth notes on the ride and some eighth-note options on the snare drum. As you develop this, work on playing the snare and bass drum notes softly.

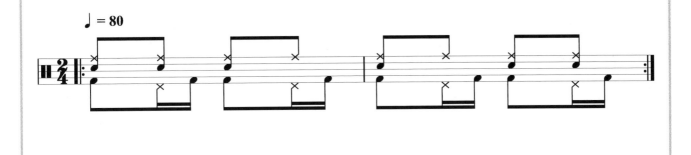

TUESDAY   135

Here, we work on placing the snare notes in different spots within the pattern, similar to some of the previous Bossa Nova patterns.

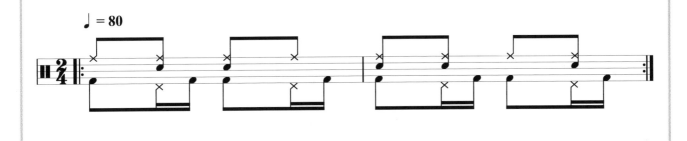

This pattern works in some different options on the snare. Start focusing on increasing your tempo and pay attention to the aforementioned dynamics.

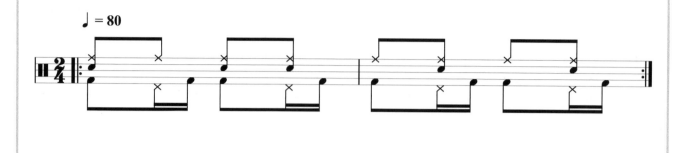

Sixteenth notes get deployed here, which is a new element for you in playing this style. Make sure to keep the snare drum on the softer side.

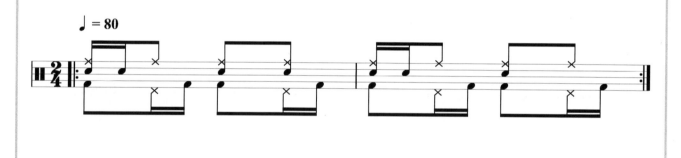

As we continue to explore 16th notes, remember that you can also play all of these patterns as a cross-stick groove or combine cross stick with regular snare hits.

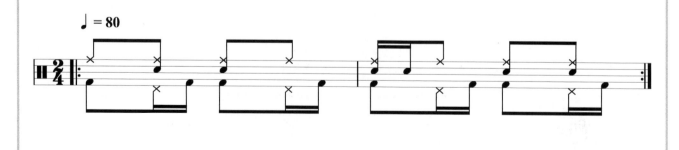

Pattern 139 is a bit tougher, with more notes on the snare, but you have already seen this in the Afrobeat section. So, if you approach this pattern with the same level of detail, it should come together nicely.

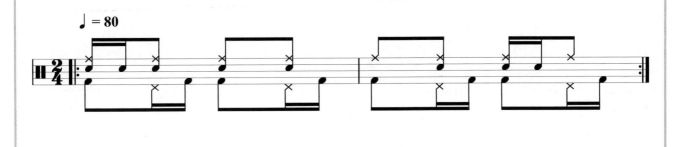

The last groove for this week follows suit with the others. By this point, you should be paying closer attention to the dynamics and also pushing the tempo up. If, however, you are not ready to handle all of that, don't force it! Be patient—it will come to you in time.

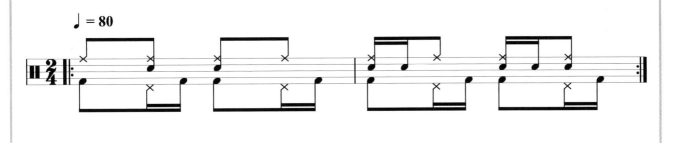

SUGGESTED LISTENING AND PLAY-ALONGS:
- "Magalenha" Sergio Mendes
- "Samba de Orfeu" Cal Tjader
- "Alvorada" Cartola
- "Trem Das Onze" Adoniran Barbosa
- "Samba Da Benção" Bebel Gilberto

NOTABLE DRUMMERS:
- Harvey Mason
- Grady Tate
- Walfredo Reyes Jr.
- Billy Higgins
- João Parahyba

WEEK 21: BLUES 2

Our second week of blues adds a few more elements to the style, including changing up the bass drum and a few different things on the snare. Between this week and the previous blues week, you should have a good bit of information on playing this style. The final, and most important, steps are to listen to it extensively and play it with other musicians, as there is no substitute for that interaction.

MONDAY   141

The first groove this week is a hard-driving blues groove that works out the bass drum. This type of pattern is useful for pushing up the energy in a rock-oriented blues song.

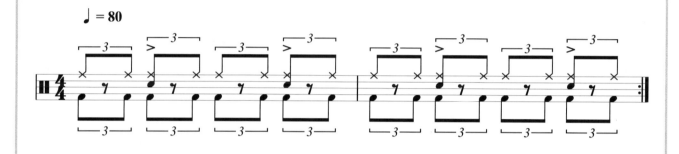

TUESDAY   142

Pattern 142 incorporates some ghost notes on the snare for this half-time feel, which is in the vein of the "Purdie Shuffle," made famous by Bernard Purdie. There are many examples of this groove in songs by Purdie and other drummers. Be sure to play the ghost notes as quiet as possible while playing the accented notes solidly.

WEDNESDAY

This groove is a straight-eighth-note, early rock 'n' roll groove that Earl Palmer pioneered with Little Richard. It was very common in the '50s and shows up regularly in the blues. This pattern is challenging to play dynamically, so it's very important to listen to recordings to hear the feel, which is a bit "slippery" and not at all rigid.

THURSDAY

Pattern 144 adds some different accents and bass drum notes to the groove. Try to add just a bit of swing to the feel, as it resides somewhere between a straight feel and a swung feel, which is tricky to assimilate.

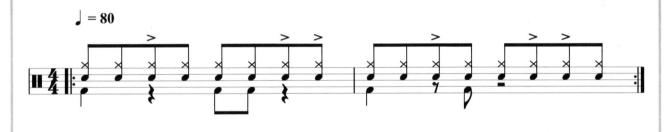

FRIDAY

Pattern 145 follows the Purdie Shuffle-style groove but adds more notes on the bass drum, which shuffles the groove a bit more, taking it in more than one direction.

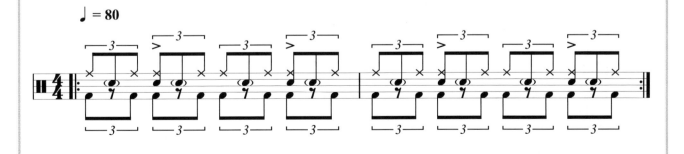

SATURDAY

The "Rock Shuffle" turns up next. Here, we shuffle the snare, ride, and bass drum all together. This, of course, can be done in blues but is heard more often in rock and metal styles. You can accent all the components on beats 2 and 4 to drive this feel.

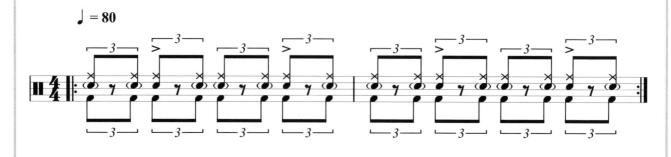

SUNDAY

The closing groove mixes up elements of the half-time feel with some different bass drum patterns across the two-measure phrase. You may need to take each measure at a time before you assemble it completely.

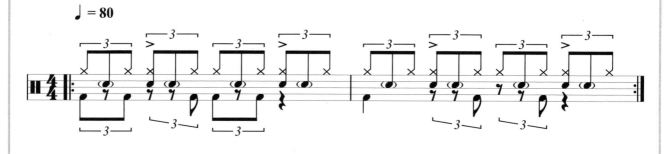

SUGGESTED LISTENING AND PLAY-ALONGS:
- "Hit the Road Jack" Ray Charles
- "Lucille" Little Richard
- "Babylon Sisters" Steely Dan
- "Born Under a Bad Sign" Albert King
- "I'd Rather Go Blind" Etta James

NOTABLE DRUMMERS:
- Chris Layton
- Al Jackson Jr.
- Howard Grimes
- Clifton James
- Tom Hambridge

WEEK 22: FUNK 2

Our second week of funk brings us more work with ghost notes, varying hi-hat rhythms, as well as some opens with the hi-hat. This all adds more overall complexity to each pattern, so I encourage you to work in layers. For example, get the basics of the pattern together first, then add the ghost notes, then the opens of the hi-hat (when used), and, lastly, any accents that are notated.

MONDAY   148

We start this section with the hi-hat only on the "ands" of each beat. This will create some space in the groove and bring out the other notes nicely. Make sure you count through each measure completely.

TUESDAY   149

Pay attention to the accents in this pattern and the counting, especially in measure 2, where there is no note on beat 1. That space may throw you off, as the bass drum hits with the hi-hat on the "and," which can make it feel like the "one" moved. Counting will keep you on track.

WEDNESDAY

Here, we begin to add some hi-hat opens. As we get into more intricate note combinations, try to remember that note dynamics has more to do with making a groove "funky" than how much you can fit into a bar. In this style, feel is literally everything, so studying the examples and drummers will help you greatly.

THURSDAY

Pattern 151 mixes hi-hat opens with some 16ths and eighths, which, at first, may feel random to you. Work up the hi-hat first and then, when you get it under control and the pattern internalized, add the snare and bass.

FRIDAY

Ghost notes, hi-hat opens, accents, and mixed note combinations make this pattern tricky, so go slowly. Also, remember to barely lifting your stick for the ghost notes, which will help you control the volume easier.

Straight 16th notes on the hi-hat can be tough, so make sure you're relaxed when you practice this pattern, and work the tempo up slowly. The hi-hat is designed to be played with one hand but that gets more difficult at faster tempos.

This pattern is like yesterday's but has just one open hi-hat (bar 2). Sometimes a subtle change can add a lot but be tough to lock in. As you play these grooves, make sure you're not sounding rigid. Record yourself so you can hear what your feel sounds like and then compare it to the recordings below.

SUGGESTED LISTENING AND PLAY-ALONGS:
- "If You Want Me to Stay" Sly & the Family Stone
- "Rock Steady" Aretha Franklin
- "Just the Way You Are" Bruno Mars
- "Kissing My Love" Bill Withers
- "I Got the Feeling" James Brown

NOTABLE DRUMMERS:
- Andy Newmark
- Zigaboo Modeliste
- Uriel Jones
- Richard "Pistol" Allen
- Tiki Fulwood

WEEK 23: REGGAE 1

Week 23 features the reggae style. The approach to this music is very unique and our first step into playing grooves that have emphasis within the measure that is different from what we are used to with other styles. Often, the grooves are rooted in a half-time triplet feel, but this week, we will focus on grooves with straight eighth notes. The element most critical to this style is the accent on beat 3 (the "drop"). This week, we will focus on that and different placements of the cross stick. You can replace the cross stick with the snare but you should be comfortable using both. Reggae originated in Jamaica and was pioneered by Bob Marley but there have been many other great reggae artists, some of whom are listed in the listening sections.

MONDAY   155

Our first reggae pattern is a stripped-down groove. Use this pattern to focus on the dynamics of the style and to capture the drop, making sure that it comes through clearly and strongly.

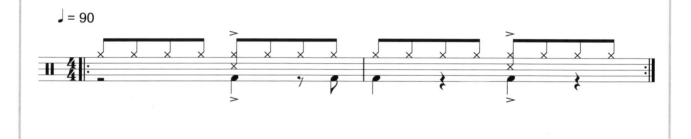

TUESDAY   156

Pattern 156 brings in some new cross-stick notes. Again, make sure the drop stands out from the other notes. You can also play the drop on the snare but the cross stick is very common.

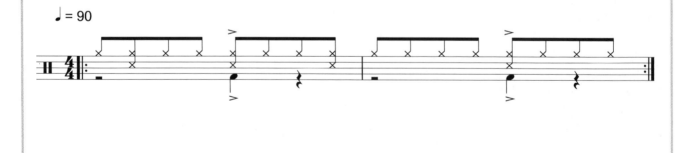

WEDNESDAY

We strip away the majority of the notes for this pattern, so focus on the feel and, when you're comfortable with it, push up the tempo a bit to get an idea of what it sounds like at a faster speed.

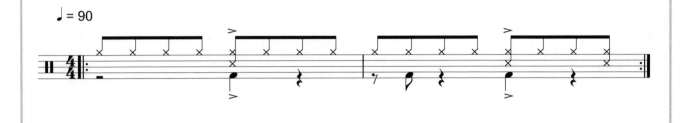

THURSDAY

Pattern 158 incorporates more notes on the bass drum and cross stick, which makes emphasizing the drop a little more difficult, so you'll probably want to work the groove up in sections.

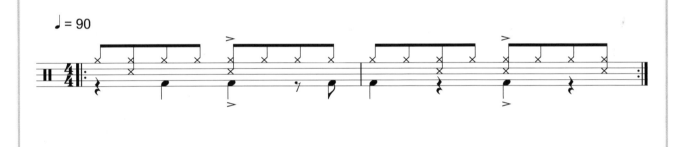

FRIDAY

This groove lands many of the cross stick and bass drum notes at the same time, which makes emphasizing the drop more difficult because you have to fight the urge to play *all* of those notes louder.

SATURDAY

One of the tricky things about reggae is that so many of the notes on cross stick and bass drum are in unusual places—at least what is common to other styles. This pattern has many of the notes in those unorthodox spots.

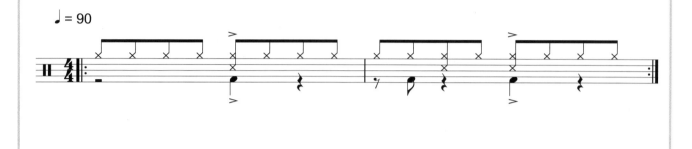

SUNDAY

The last pattern for this week has a string of bass drum notes in the second bar, which is a bit tricky. As usual, work it up in pieces so that you're not forcing it.

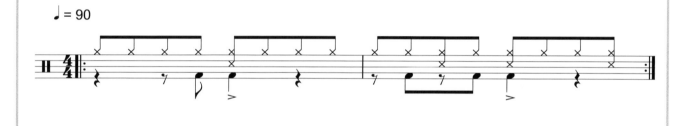

SUGGESTED LISTENING AND PLAY-ALONGS:
- "One Love" Bob Marley
- "Walking on the Moon" The Police
- "Croaking Lizard" Lee Perry and the Upsetters
- "Engine 54" The Ethiopians
- "Book of Rules" The Heptones

NOTABLE DRUMMERS:
- Sly Dunbar
- Carlton Barrett
- Winston Grennan
- Uziah Thompson
- Alvin Patterson

WEEK 24: LINEAR FILLS 2

This week, we will spend some more time on linear fills. The fills here use triplet combinations and are written to be played with rock beats but can be applied to any style of music as fills and/or grooves. Indeed, many drummers have used this approach to devise some very interesting groove ideas. Once you have the coordinations sorted, move your hands to different surfaces, which will give you some interesting combinations.

MONDAY   162

This first groove is a common linear fill that appears in many different styles of music. Make sure that you keep the notes even, which can be tough to do when they are spread across hi-hat, snare, and bass drum. The dynamics can be tricky to get under control to maintain the triplet sound.

TUESDAY   163

If you play Pattern 163 while keeping your hands on each sound source, the pattern's lead hand will naturally flip. You don't have to play it that way but I recommend that you at least try it that way before mixing up the sticking.

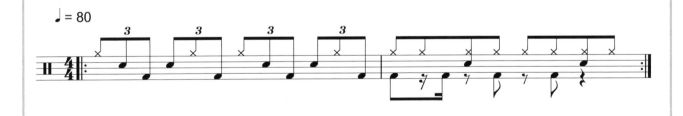

WEDNESDAY

This pattern leads with the bass drum and then the snare, putting the hi-hat note in the middle of each triplet. This is a good exercise for your weak hand and great for developing your balance.

THURSDAY

When working up this fill, I recommend playing each surface with one hand, which is a return to the doubled triplet that we saw a few weeks ago. Also, as with all of these patterns, you can move your hands to the toms and cymbals to see what different sounds you can generate.

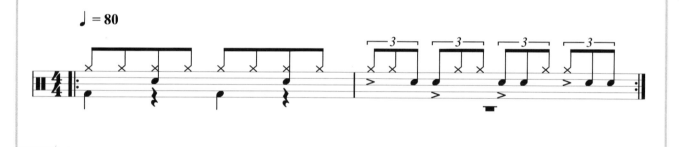

FRIDAY

Pattern 166 puts the hi-hat in the middle of the triplet again, but this time with the bass drum on the first note and the snare on the last. This pattern has a good flow to it, as the bass drum essentially functions as a quarter-note feel, which propels the fill.

SATURDAY

Sixteenth-note triplets are the focus of this fill. If you have a hard time with the tempo, then pull everything way back and work it up slowly so that it flows well. Then, when you're ready, move your hands around the kit, as this will render many options.

SUNDAY

The first measure of Pattern 168 mixes 16th notes phrased in groups of 3 with the snare on beat 4 in a backbeat manner. The second measure features eighth-note triplets broken up in the same way. This is a good exercise for working back-and-forth between 16ths and triplets in a groove setting. This isn't the most practical pattern but it can help to improve your timing comprehension.

SUGGESTED LISTENING AND PLAY-ALONGS:
- "Cissy Strut" The Meters
- "Oakland Stroke" Tower of Power
- "Where Are You Going" Dave Matthews Band
- "Everybody Wants Some" Galactic
- "Come Together" The Beatles

NOTABLE DRUMMERS:
- Mike Clark
- Bill Bruford
- Vinnie Colaiuta
- Carter Beauford
- Stewart Copeland

WEEK 25: METAL 2

This second week of metal patterns adds some fill ideas and triplet-style grooves. As you lock these down, drive the tempos up so you can hear the beats in a setting that might be more recognizable to your ears. Always make sure that you are solid at slower tempos first because rushing things will usually just bring sloppiness and control issues. Again, if you're not a double-bass player, then skip this week.

MONDAY 169

A single string of triplets is the focus of this week's first pattern. You can play these with either foot leading but I do recommend that you play them with alternate strokes at first, and then try different combinations.

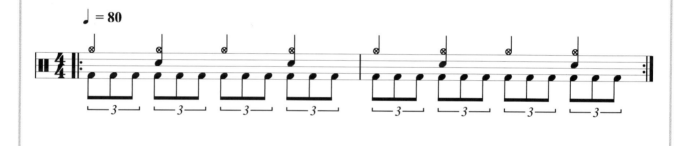

TUESDAY 170

An extra snare hit on the back end of the triplets on beats 2 and 4 are what differentiate this pattern from the previous one. The snare and bass notes should line up cleanly and stay that way as you work up speed.

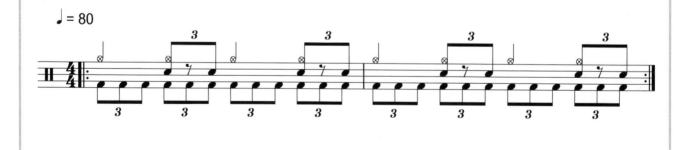

WEDNESDAY

Pattern 171 works as a fill or groove, although you can certainly move your hands to the toms, cymbals, or whatever you choose to hit, if you get comfortable with it.

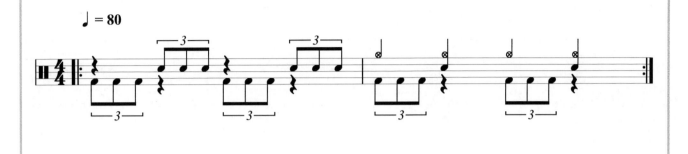

THURSDAY

In measure 2, we break up a string of 16th notes into two groups of 6 and then a group of 4 to finish with your hands. There are many interesting ways to cut up a sequence of 16th notes—just count, and you'll be able to devise your own combinations.

FRIDAY

Pattern 173 uses 16th notes in the beat part (bar 1) and then breaks them up in a common way for the fill (bar 2). Again, there are many ways to approach this type of pattern but you can use this one as a starting point; just make sure your notes are even when you're playing these combinations, as they will be easier to hear in the music you're performing.

This groove breaks up the 16ths and also goes into a pattern that is in the vein of a "blast beat." This pattern is common in many kinds of metal and is one that is played at extremely high speeds, so consistent, even, controlled repetition will get you on the right path.

The last pattern for this week can be played many different ways, so find the approach that works for you and go with it. If you're unsure, then a safe bet is to use alternate strokes and work that up to speed. That is always a great way to approach this material, as it will develop your balance first, and when you get proficient, you can try new things.

SUGGESTED LISTENING AND PLAY-ALONGS:
- "Where Eagles Dare" Iron Maiden
- "The Motherload" Mastodon
- "Toxicity" System of a Down
- "Coming Undone" Korn
- "Stricken" Disturbed

NOTABLE DRUMMERS:
- Tommy Lee
- Darby Todd
- Dave Lombardo
- Vinnie Paul
- Lars Ulrich

WEEK 26: REVIEW 2

Our second review week is a bit more challenging, as we are getting deeper into styles. If you're comfortable, try to drive towards the tempos that are listed with each pattern. If you weren't able to get these grooves up to that speed the first time, go for it now.

MONDAY 176

Pattern 176 is an Afrobeat groove. You should be a bit more comfortable with notes in different spots, so this groove should be easier than when you first tried it. If it isn't, be patient with yourself—it will come back to you if you ease into it.

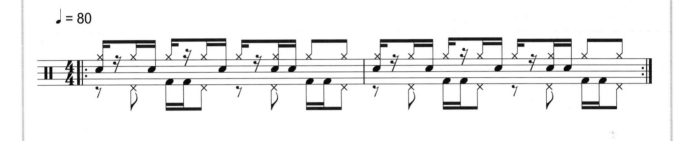

TUESDAY 177

Next up is a linear fill that's fun to move around the kit.

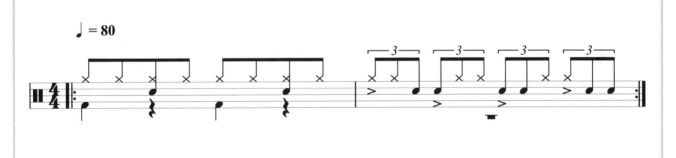

WEDNESDAY

Funk comes next in this review. Here, we revisit the off-beat hi-hat pattern. Be sure to note the ghost notes and accents, as they add a lot to the flow of this groove.

THURSDAY

Pattern 179 is a Samba groove. If you can't get to full speed yet, no big deal. Work towards it over time and make sure that you keep a relaxed feel going throughout.

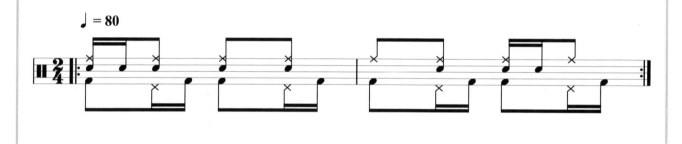

FRIDAY

Double bass shows up in this metal pattern. If you skipped this section, then grab a pattern from another week of your choice to review. Aim for something that you need to work on, as that will benefit you the most. That said, if you're reviewing this pattern, then make sure all of your notes are coming across cleanly and clearly.

SATURDAY

Pattern 181 is a swing ostinato from Week 19 and is great for flipping your lead hands in the vein of a paradiddle. As you push the tempo, work some bounce/rebound on the doubles or control the second note with your fingers.

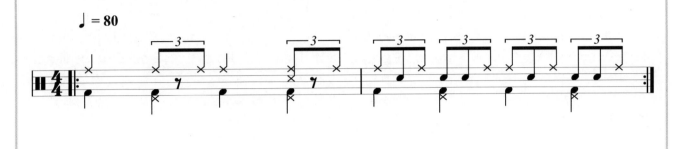

SUNDAY

Our last review pattern works 16th notes in the snare and bass drum against eighth-note hi-hats. Keep your hat hand steady as the other notes move against it through the measure.

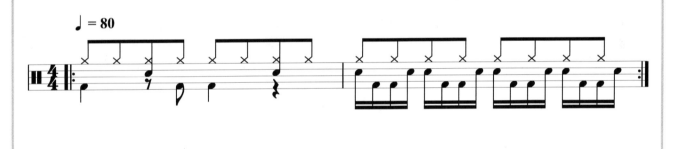

WEEK 27: NEW ORLEANS 1

We shift gears now to a totally fresh approach to drumming, New Orleans/Second Line grooves. These are some of the slinkiest feels you will ever come across and assimilating the subtlety of this style takes a lot of listening. For the most part, you'll be playing two hands on the snare and have a series of accents to deal with throughout each pattern while also dealing with some coordination challenges in the foot patterns. You will find some similarities to the Bossa Nova and Samba, as well as the upcoming Baião, but through listening, you will hear differences. Keep in mind that the pattens you will see in this book for this style are not the end-all, be-all; there are many ways to interpret this style, as well as lots of patterns from other styles that can be assimilated into this fun approach to drumming.

MONDAY
183

Our first pattern this week uses pedaled hi-hats on the "ands" of every beat and accents with your hands on the snare. Keep the groove loose and "swampy" to capture the feel of this style.

TUESDAY
184

As with the last groove, the bass drum pattern is a bit tricky underneath the snare accents. You may need to work the bass drum and hi-hat in isolation before you tackle the hands.

WEDNESDAY

Watch out for this pattern and the ostinato in the feet. If you struggle, apply the same approach to it as you did to the Bossa and Samba (i.e., getting the feet locked in first).

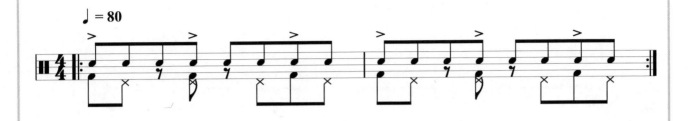

THURSDAY

Pattern 186 is a common groove. Again, try not to play it rigidly; instead, keep a looseness to the feel. That said, learn it the way that works best for you, focusing on the feel of it later if you need to.

FRIDAY

If you're struggling with assimilating the feel of this style, don't be afraid to back up to an earlier groove, one that enables you to concentrate on the sound and feel of this style.

SATURDAY

Pattern 188 uses some buzz rolls at the end of measure 2. This is a staple of this style of drumming. If you're unfamiliar with roll techniques, then I suggest you review some snare studies. The buzz roll techniques for New Orleans/Second Line are similar to traditional methods but you need to adapt them to this style of music and its flow.

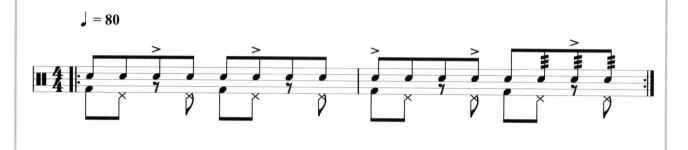

SUNDAY

This week's final groove uses a 2-3 clave pattern on the bass drum, which may be difficult for you at first. Break the groove down to the feet for a bit and then add the hands when you have the control sorted. Be patient with this one if it's tough for you.

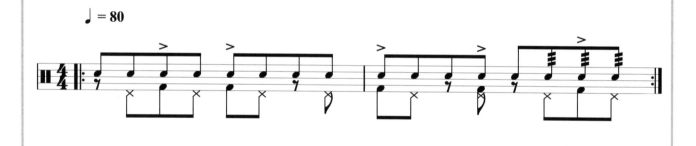

SUGGESTED LISTENING AND PLAY-ALONGS:
- "Hey Pocky A-Way" The Meters
- "Big Chief" Professor Longhair
- "Iko Iko" Dr. John
- "All on Mardi Gras Day" The Wild Magnolias
- "Lagniappe Part 2" Trombone Shorty

NOTABLE DRUMMERS:
- Johnny Vidacovich
- Zigaboo Modeliste
- Stanton Moore
- Herman Ernest
- Russell Batiste Jr.

WEEK 28: BEBOP 1

As we crest the halfway point of this material, we begin to work on some more independence. Bebop is a vast, deep style of drumming that, like many of the styles in this book, warrants a book of study unto itself to get you to a high skill level. There is a lot more to playing this style than just working up patterns, as comprehension of song forms and melody will really help you to understand how to apply these coordinations musically.

The main difference between bebop and swing is that the bass drum moves away from the traditional four beats to the bar and instead becomes more active, much like a hand. Your ability to hold the ride pattern is important to developing your independence. When playing with others, however, the ride pattern is your choice and should be phrased in whatever way makes the most musical sense. In other words, it doesn't have to be beholden to the pattern that is notated or commonly used.

MONDAY   190

Our first bebop pattern saves the bass drum for the very end of the sequence. This is part of what sets this approach to jazz apart from swing, but the work you have been doing up to this point is prepping you to handle this level of independence. Work it slowly.

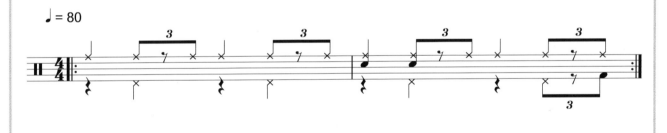

TUESDAY   191

Here, we gradually start to add more notes to the bass drum. Note that, when you're working these up, some notes align with the ride pattern and some don't. That may help you while putting this coordination together.

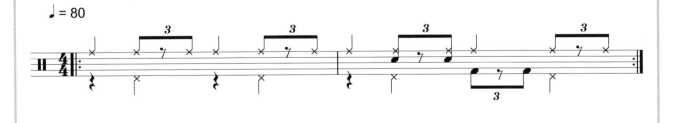

WEDNESDAY

Pattern 192 adds more notes to the snare, which may get tricky. Once you get those in place, you should be able to add the bass drum.

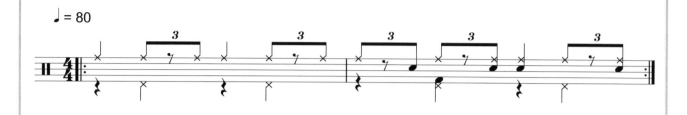

THURSDAY

We've been adding notes to different spots but, by now, you should have the necessary independence to drop those in without too much trouble.

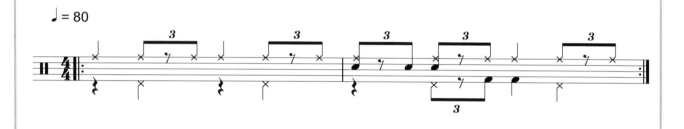

FRIDAY

Pattern 194 flips the snare and bass notes so the groove feels "upside down," depending on how you're feeling it.

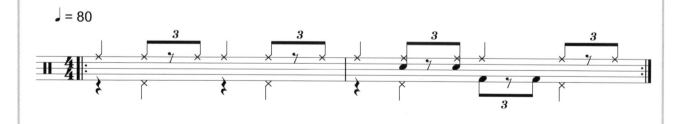

SATURDAY

More bass drum notes are added to Pattern 195, so be sure to get them into the right spots. Also, count and go slow enough so you can process all of the information.

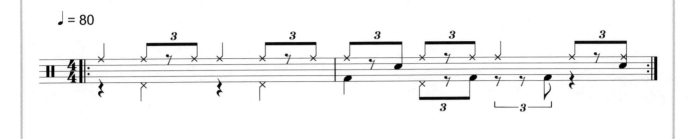

SUNDAY

The last pattern for this week is a full two-measure phrase. It may take a bit to assimilate all of it but, for the most part, the notes and positions should be familiar.

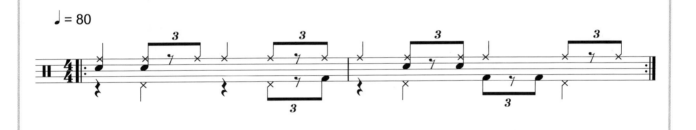

SUGGESTED LISTENING AND PLAY-ALONGS:
- "So What" Miles Davis
- "Moanin'" Art Blakey
- "Half Nelson" Charlie Parker
- "Hot House" Dizzy Gillespie
- "Straight, No Chaser" Thelonious Monk

NOTABLE DRUMMERS:
- Max Roach
- Kenny Clarke
- Roy Haynes
- Philly Joe Jones
- Art Blakey

WEEK 29: SAMBA OSTINATOS

The third week of ostinato exercises gets you working the hands over the top of Samba foot patterns. This can be very challenging, so pace yourself and try not to force it. We use 16th notes at first, but these patterns can be played with all kinds of different notes and variations—this is just the first step.

MONDAY   197

Pattern 197 is basically alternate-stroke 16ths on the snare, but after you get this down, move it around the kit. Of course, you can change the sticking to whatever you prefer.

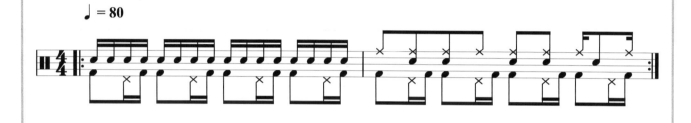

TUESDAY   198

This pattern is doubles back and forth on each hand, which may feel strange against the Samba, so make sure the notes line up and don't rush it.

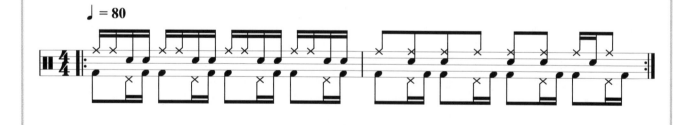

WEDNESDAY

Pattern 199 is a reversal of yesterday's pattern, so your lead hand will flip. Whether you choose to use alternate sticking or mix it up, you will discover new things and the positions of the notes against the feet will move.

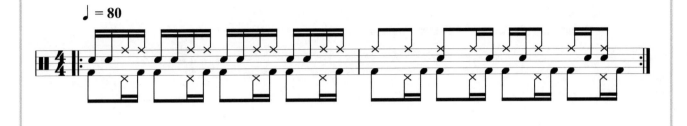

THURSDAY

Here, the doubles work across each beat, which may feel odd to you at first, but this is a great exercise for getting comfortable with the coordination required for the Samba and Baião grooves later in the book.

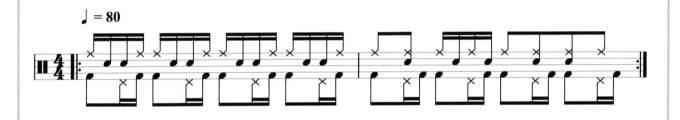

FRIDAY

Pattern 201 reverses the direction of the previous pattern. It may feel completely new to you but don't get flustered—this just means a weakness in your coordination is being revealed, one that needs to be addressed.

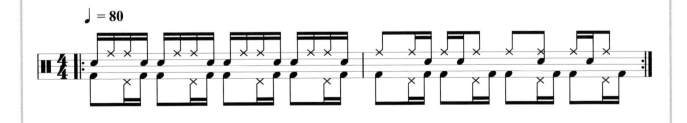

SATURDAY

This pattern marks the return of our old friend the paradiddle, in this case working against the Samba. This is a wonderful workout for your coordination and will open doors for upcoming work.

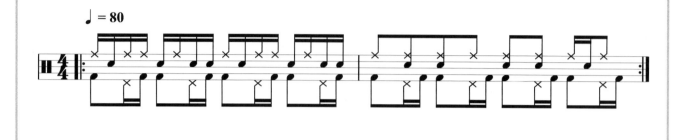

SUNDAY

Pattern 203 is a paradiddle-type sticking combination that can be performed many different ways but play it as written first to maximize the benefits of pushing your coordination.

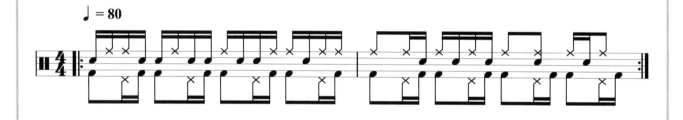

SUGGESTED LISTENING AND PLAY-ALONGS:
- "Samba De Flora" Airto
- "Ah, Rio" Ron Carter
- "One Note Samba" Herbie Mann
- "Tim Tim Por Tim Tim" Milton Banana Trio
- "Don't Want to Be a Part of Your World" David Byrne

NOTABLE DRUMMERS:
- Milton Banana
- Cyro Baptista
- Edison Machado
- Dom Um Romão
- Naná Vasconcelos

WEEK 30: AFROBEAT 2

Afrobeat 2 gets into some more detailed coordination with the left hand and some additional movement in the bass drum. This style doesn't have a lot of fill-oriented content. Although fills can certainly be included, they aren't quite as important as the groove, which is intended to be more trance-like, requiring lots of repetition, and songs can go on for extended lengths of time, so locking in a great feel with subtle embellishment is important.

MONDAY   204

Our first groove starts with the snare and bass drum inverted, so be ready for that. Having different rhythms coming from lots of sources is a common element in Afrobeat. Listening to the song examples will teach you a lot about how the drum set fits into this style, as it needs to integrate organically and not dominate the sonic space.

TUESDAY   205

Pattern 205 returns to some familiar rhythms from the first week of Afrobeat, except now we add two more 16th notes to beat 4.

WEDNESDAY

We invert again for this pattern. Watch for the changing hi-hat pattern, as well, including the opens that happen on beats 2 and 4.

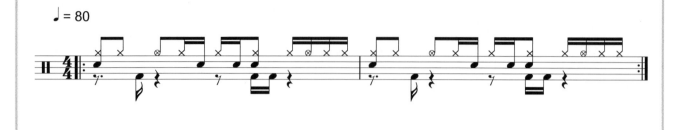

THURSDAY

There are three different hi-hat rhythms happening in this pattern, which is one of the toughest in this style. It may take you a while to put it all together. Go for the hi-hat opens only after you nail down the basic rhythms first.

FRIDAY

Some familiar notes turn up in this groove, which includes a few slight changes on the snare to differentiate it a bit from others.

In this pattern, we add one extra note to the snare to add a little fire to this groove, demonstrating that just one note change can make a difference in how a groove sounds.

Pattern 210 may be the oddest-sounding of these grooves. Again, the hi-hat may be the trickiest part, as there are three different note combinations through each measure. Make sure those are locked in before you add the other elements.

SUGGESTED LISTENING AND PLAY-ALONGS:
- "Zombie" Fela Kuti
- "Never" Tony Allen
- "In the Middle" The Daktaris
- "Water No Get Enemy" Femi Kuti
- "Madjafalao" Le Tout-Puissant Orchestre Poly-Rythmo

NOTABLE DRUMMERS:
- Tony Allen
- Fela Kuti
- Ginger Baker
- Kevin Raczka
- Cheikh Lo

WEEK 31: ODD-TIME ROCK 1

This week, we hit the first of two weeks of odd-time rock grooves. All of these patterns have the quarter note getting the beat; the next week of odd meters will have the eighth note as the bottom number of the signature.

There are so many ways to approach odd-time music and drumming, but what we have here is an introduction to a handful of common time signatures you may come across in rock-style drumming. Make sure you count your way through the measures at first, especially if you are unfamiliar. These grooves are what I would call "skeleton" patterns, as they are just basic approaches to help you get acquainted and comfortable with new time signatures. Have fun!

MONDAY   211

3/4 time is first. If you've never played in 3/4, it may feel like your "missing something." Well, you are... one beat! Count it steady ("1, 2, 3," etc.) and you should be fine.

TUESDAY   212

The next pattern adds a few extra elements to the mix to spice up the groove a bit. Nothing unfamiliar here; just some variety.

WEDNESDAY

5/4 time is up next. This is fun because now we get into different ways we can phrase the pattern within the measure. In this case, we just add a note to the end of the groove; otherwise, this should pretty much feel like a 4/4 pattern. You can count this up to 5 or as a bar of 3 and a bar of 2.

THURSDAY

This pattern adds some more elements to the groove and pushes the snare to almost the end of the measure while also landing a few snare hits in odd-feeling places. By adding just one beat to the measure, the options for creating a beat expand considerably. Be sure to keep counting.

FRIDAY

7/4 time is next up. Now we have lots of options for counting the groove. We can count it "1, 2, 3, 4, 1, 2, 3" or reverse that. Or you can devise a system that works for you. There are no real rules on counting 7/4 other than just knowing where you are and where you're going in the measure, especially if you're playing with other musicians.

SATURDAY

A bar of 7/4 can really stretch out your options for what you can play and where you can place the notes. This example shows the snare going right to the edge of the measure to help retain the flow of the groove and take some of the "oddness" out.

SUNDAY

This last groove alternates 5/4 and 7/4. While it can certainly be thought of as 12/4, that might be more counting than you want to do, hence breaking it up.

SUGGESTED LISTENING AND PLAY-ALONGS:
- "Nothing Else Matters" Metallica (3/4)
- "Solsbury Hill" Peter Gabriel (7/4)
- "15 Step" Radiohead (5/4)
- "Fell on Black Days" Soundgarden (6/4)
- "Money" Pink Floyd (7/4)

NOTABLE DRUMMERS:
- Pat Mastelotto
- Matt Garstka
- Phil Selway
- Nick Mason
- Matt Cameron

WEEK 32: SAMBA 2

This last week of Samba introduces two new ride patterns that are very common in this style. These are basic coordinations but there is much more to still be developed. For example, you can change the ride patterns by using different ideas in place of the three we have covered. You can also phrase your snare hand with cross stick or by moving to the toms and floor tom to create a more melodic pattern. Also, you can apply rim shots and buzz notes with the left hand on the snare or elsewhere to change the sound. If you listen to traditional Samba music, which often features only drums, you will hear many incredible sounds and textures.

MONDAY   218

We use three 16th notes on the ride cymbal for this pattern, which you should be relatively familiar with by now. You may have trouble using it with the foot ostinatos but you will get it.

TUESDAY   219

Watch the snare in this and upcoming patterns, as it gets a bit trickier. If you need to, just play the hands first. That is sometimes the best way to tackle these patterns.

WEDNESDAY

As we are driving through this material, be sure to be pull back the volume of your bass drum, which will give this a lighter feel.

THURSDAY

Using the cross stick, as well as the snare, on these patterns is a good idea and will diversify your options for the groove.

FRIDAY

The snare work and off-beats get a bit more involved in Pattern 222. After you learn the notes, try to work different dynamics on the snare so it isn't always loud.

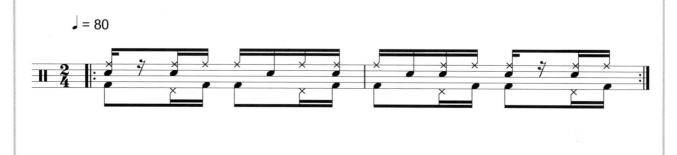

Keeping the dynamics in mind, feel free to accent different notes within this pattern. It will add layers of complexity to the groove and, more importantly, develop your dynamic control.

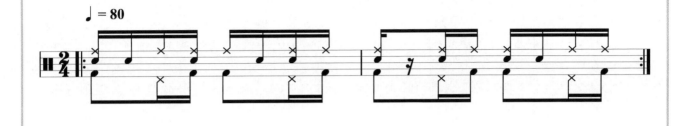

Pattern 224 features more note combinations. You can also try moving your snare hand to the toms for different sounds. You will hear that in some of the audio examples below.

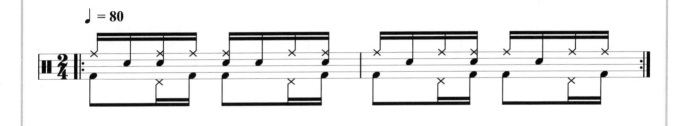

SUGGESTED LISTENING AND PLAY-ALONGS:
- "Samba Cruzado" Percussion Madness Vol. 1
- "Partido do Samba" Percussion Madness Vol. 1
- "Se é tarde me perdoa" Carlos Lyra
- "Mas, Que Nada" Jorge Ben
- "Deve Ser Amor" Baden Powell

NOTABLE DRUMMERS:
- Maria Martinez
- Roberto Pontes Dias
- Dave Bailey
- Johnny Rae
- Claudio Slon

WEEK 33: BAIÃO 1

The Baião is another Brazilian style that is similar in many ways to the Bossa Nova and Samba. The main difference is in the bass drum ostinato, where some notes are the same and some are different. After spending time working up the Samba ostinato, it may be tough to adjust to the change but apply the same discipline and patience to learning this style as you have the others and it will come together for you. This form appears frequently amongst Bossa and Samba styles, often on the same albums. Also, the bass drum pattern shows up in New Orleans Second Line grooves and has also made it into a lot of club music in the last 20 years.

MONDAY   225

We start off the Baião with some familiar rhythms on your hands so you can focus on getting the feet sorted out. If this pattern is too difficult for you at first, then you can always simplify it by taking notes out and then adding them back in when you're ready.

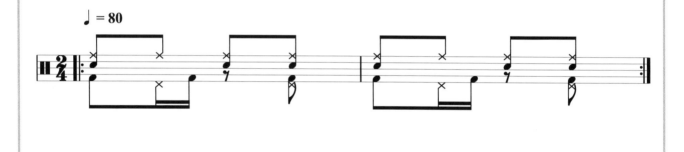

TUESDAY   226

Landing snare notes with the bass drum is sometimes tricky. When you see them here, make sure that you don't flam them too much. You want the groove to stay nice and crisp.

WEDNESDAY

Pattern 227 adds a few extra notes. By now, you should be getting a bit more settled in on the foot ostinato.

THURSDAY

A change up to three 16th notes on the ride comes next, as well as a snare pattern that is not overly busy.

FRIDAY

Here, we start to mix up the snare notes while keeping the ride pattern locked in.

By the time you hit this pattern, I'm hoping the three-16th-notes ride pattern is locking in, as you should be pretty familiar with it by now. That said, some note combinations can still pose surprising challenges.

With the last pattern of the week, we get into more off-beat notes on the snare and things are moving pretty fast. Make sure you're counting is locked in and, when you're confident, start to experiment with different sounds, as you may have done in the last Samba section.

SUGGESTED LISTENING AND PLAY-ALONGS:
- "Três E Trezentos" Luiz Gonzaga
- "Baião Destemperado" Barbatuques
- "Baião De Quatro Toques" Andrea Motis
- "Baião" Abacaxi
- "Baião em Howth" Igor Brasil

NOTABLE DRUMMERS:
- Guegué Medeiros
- Airto Moreira
- Wilson das Neves
- Michael Shrieve

WEEK 34: REGGAE 2

Reggae 2 introduces triplets on the hi-hat. This is a very popular way to phrase in this style and is common in many songs. Keep laying the accent on beat 3 like before and gradually add the new elements when you feel comfortable. These patterns are notated with either the snare or the cross stick but you should be able to work comfortably between both sounds.

MONDAY   232

Here, the triplet feel shows up on the hi-hat. This pattern is a reggae staple that you will hear in many songs. You can sub out the cross stick for a hit on the snare if you like.

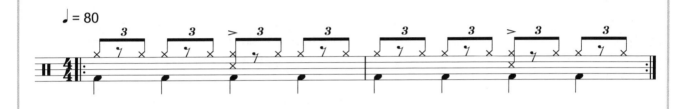

TUESDAY   233

Pattern 233 breaks up the hi-hat pattern, playing it like a swing ride pattern. Be sure to land all the accents in the right spot, as it makes a big difference in capturing the feel.

WEDNESDAY

Pattern 234 breaks up the triplet feel and is an example of how it can be re-phrased in many different ways. You may need to lock the hands in first before adding the bass drum.

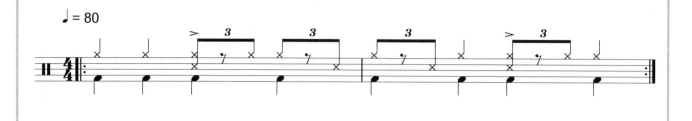

THURSDAY

235

We add quarter-note triplets to Pattern 235 and drop in the snare drum, which, of course, can also be played as a cross stick. You may need to play just the hi-hat and bass drum together to lock in the polyrhythm.

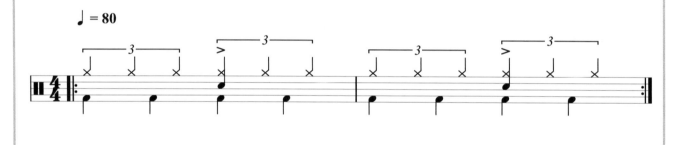

FRIDAY

236

Pattern 236 mixes quarter-note and eighth-note triplets, giving us a fresh take on the feel and another common way to phrase the groove.

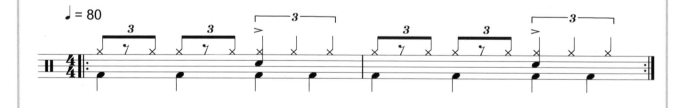

Here, the triplet pattern is broken up even further but the constant is the snare drop on beat 3. That cannot be stressed enough.

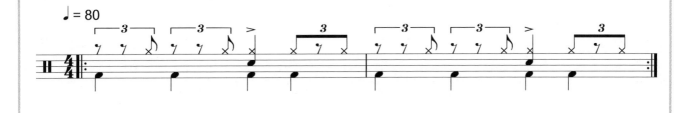

Pattern 238 breaks up our hi-hat one more time, giving us more fresh ways to approach the groove. Remember, all of these examples can be taken in many directions but the drop on beat 3 should stay prominent and consistent in your groove. You can play all around it creatively but should strive to make it happen in every measure.

SUGGESTED LISTENING AND PLAY-ALONGS:
- "Funkey Funkey Reggay" The Skatalites
- "Funky Kingston" Toots & the Maytals
- "Wonderful World, Beautiful People" Jimmy Cliff
- "People Funny Boy" Lee "Scratch" Perry
- "Return of Django" The Upsetters

NOTABLE DRUMMERS:
- Carlton "Santa" Davis
- Lloyd Knibb
- Gil Sharone
- Nelson Miller
- Stewart Copeland

WEEK 35: MAMBO 1

Afro-Cuban styles are some of the most difficult to get together and master. Like Brazilian styles, most originated on percussion instruments and then were adapted, in different forms, to drum set. This style is very deep, and there is a lot that can be developed, but we will work through some Mambo essentials to give you some idea as to how to approach this style and other Afro-Cuban styles. If you like this material, I highly suggest digging deeper, as there are some great books out there. Lastly, be aware of the clave patterns as you work through the material.

MONDAY   239

3-2 son clave on cross stick is where we begin our Mambo studies. The foot ostinato tends to be the issue for most people, so work that up with the ride and then try adding the cross stick.

TUESDAY   240

2-3 son clave on cross stick is the reversal of yesterday's pattern. You might think flipping the pattern will be easy, but sometimes it can be a challenge.

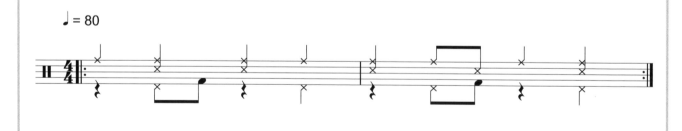

WEDNESDAY

3-2 rhumba clave is next, which is one note different from the son clave, but that one note changes the feel of the style considerably, so it's important to be accurate with this change-up.

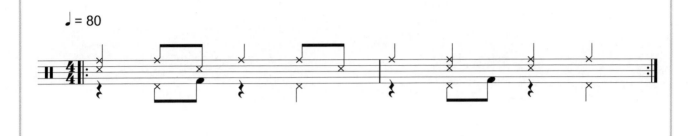

THURSDAY

We reverse the pattern again, now playing a 2-3 rhumba clave for Pattern 242. If you're struggling with this material in any way, take your time—don't force it. Sometimes hanging with a pattern for an extra day or two makes a big difference overall.

FRIDAY

Now we change up the ride pattern and return to 3-2 son clave.

SATURDAY

2-3 son clave is back again. You should be noticing an expansion in your independence as you work through this style. Each new twist can pose new difficulties with this style of music/drumming.

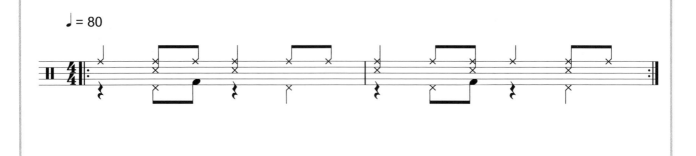

SUNDAY

We change to 3-2 rhumba clave for this one to set you up for dealing with it in the second Mambo section. As always, be sure to study the music by listening to and watching others play it. It will take some time and patience to assimilate this style into your musical world.

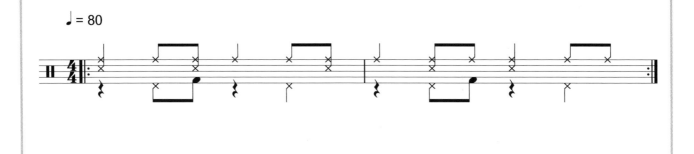

SUGGESTED LISTENING AND PLAY-ALONGS:
- "Mambo Inn" Machito
- "Afro Blue" Mongo Santamaria
- "Chekere que son" Irakere
- "Ran Kan Kan" Tito Puente
- "Manteca Theme" Dizzy Gillespie

NOTABLE DRUMMERS:
- Tito Puente
- Mongo Santamaría
- Charlie Persip
- Horacio Hernandez
- Walfredo Reyes Jr.

WEEK 36: NEW ORLEANS 2

The second week of New Orleans grooves applies some new elements to the patterns. This style of drumming requires lots of listening to grasp the subtle complexities within the patterns and how they can evolve throughout the course of a song. The patterns included here represent a very basic cross section of options but, as with most all of these styles, there is much more to learn.

MONDAY

Our first pattern starts where we left off—buzz rolls. Make sure they are loose and flowing.

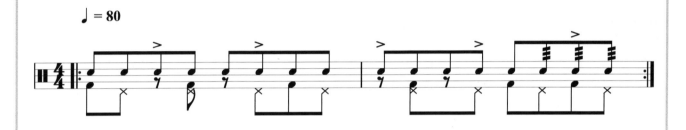

TUESDAY

Like yesterday's pattern, we have a slightly different bass drum part happening here. And some fresh accents make things a bit trickier in this pattern.

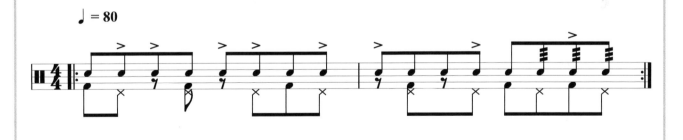

WEDNESDAY

Pattern 248 features accents and slightly different note-spacing on the bass drum but no buzzes this time.

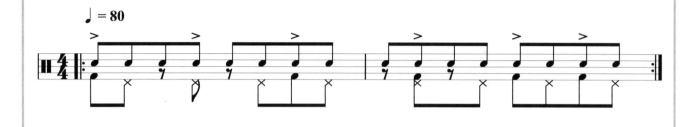

THURSDAY

Pattern 249 adds some space to the groove and brings us back to the buzzes. This pattern is particularly funky.

FRIDAY

We have buzz roll overload in Pattern 250. Try to keep the buzzes flowing, as you should feel the separate rolls—they shouldn't sound like one long, unbroken roll. However, the subdivisions notated on each beat should be implied, not played overtly clean. It's not easy to assimilate these buzz rolls without proper listening and study.

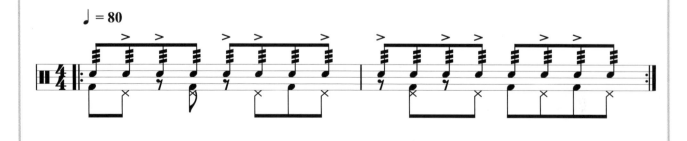

SATURDAY

Pattern 251 has a sparser bass drum part and lots of accents but no buzzes.

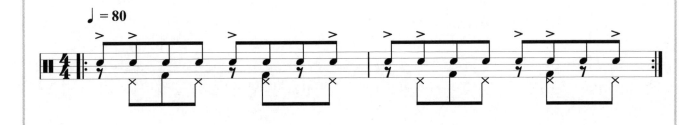

SUNDAY

This week's final pattern features a combination of accents in the first measure and buzzes in the second. There is a lot going on here, so one measure at a time might be the best way to attack it. Of course, you can also just separate limbs in any way you feel comfortable.

SUGGESTED LISTENING AND PLAY-ALONGS:
- "Mardi Gras Mambo" The Meters
- "Mardi Gras Day" Kermit Ruffins
- "I Feel Like Funkin' It Up" Rebirth Brass Band
- "It's All Over Now" Dirty Dozen Brass Band
- "Baker's Dozen" Galactic

NOTABLE DRUMMERS:
- Charles "Hungry" Williams
- Idris Muhammad
- Joseph "Smokey" Johnson
- Earl Palmer
- John Boudreaux

We deviate from style-based playing this week to focus on most people's weakest limb. The hi-hat foot is often the most neglected limb of a drum-set player, usually because... well, it doesn't operate a drum. Ironically, though, the hi-hat is the most dynamic part of the kit. We can shape the sound considerably with the pedal while we hit it or with different velocities and releases when it's closed. Control over your hi-hat can provide increased levels of dynamic control, which will allow you to shape and accent many different styles of music.

This week's patterns are a starting point but you could take this work to many different levels. Applying patterns from books like *Stick Control*, *Master Studies*, or *Syncopation* to these hi-hat patterns will present all kinds of challenges and push you to new levels of coordination and creativity. These patterns are only hi-hat closes with your foot in different parts of the measure, with a few variations in your hands over the top. Again, this is just the beginning. The suggested listening has a few examples of how players use the hi-hat as a steady rhythm for soloing or keeping time.

MONDAY   253

The first pattern puts the hi-hat on the "and' of every beat. Sometimes just playing a steady string of eighth notes or 16th notes over the top while you play the hi-hat is a good way to get oriented. But you can try different things.

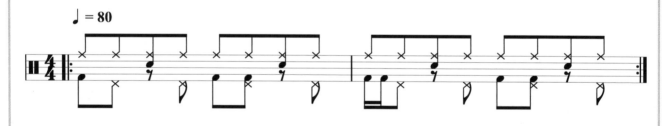

TUESDAY   254

The snare and bass drum get a bit more complex in this pattern, which again features the hi-hat on the "and." You can work beat by beat while sorting the coordination or, like I have mentioned repeatedly, one layer at a time or in combinations.

WEDNESDAY

Here, we play four quarter notes through each measure, which might be an endurance issue for you at first. If so, go slow.

THURSDAY

Switch the ride up to the familiar three-16th-notes pattern and play eighth notes in the hi-hat and see how your groove expands.

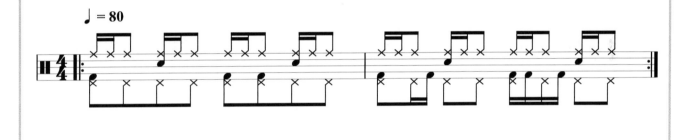

FRIDAY

Pattern 257 pulls back to quarter notes on the ride, which will allow you to really hear the eighths on the hi-hat and what a difference it can make in the sound of the kit.

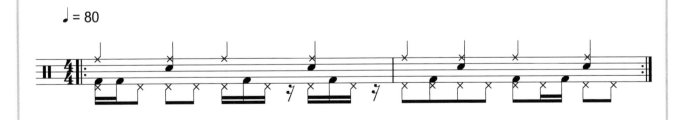

We go to another familiar broken three-16th-notes groove for Pattern 258. This, combined with the hi-hat on the "ands," can really be a fun groove to play. Try playing just the ride hand and hi-hat together at first to hear how it sounds.

Pattern 259 is a combo groove with a quarter-note ride in measure 1, followed by an offbeat ride (the "ands") in measure 2. This may seem redundant but the point is to see what happens when you layer certain sounds together and to hear the space that it creates in the groove.

SUGGESTED LISTENING AND PLAY-ALONGS:
- "The Drum Also Waltzes" Max Roach
- "Blue Wind" Jeff Beck
- "Nefertiti" Miles Davis
- "Wondering" Wolfgang Muthspiel, Scott Colley & Brian Blade
- "New Lost World" Chris Whitley

NOTABLE DRUMMERS:
- Lenny White
- Max Roach
- John Bonham
- Roy Haynes
- Matt Chamberlain

WEEK 38: REVIEW 3

The third review revisits some odd-time signatures, reggae, bebop, and New Orleans grooves. Tempos increase but only do so if you feel comfortable. Take your time and make sure you're not forcing anything.

MONDAY

The first pattern is a New Orleans groove. Like all of the patterns in this review, it's played at a faster tempo. Keep the accents clean.

TUESDAY

Reggae is next. This pattern features some mixed cross-stick rhythms, so make sure that the drop accent on beat 3 remains prominent.

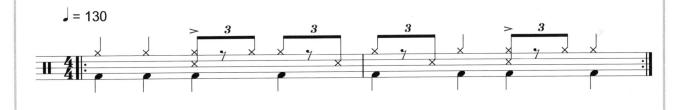

WEDNESDAY

This odd-time groove is in 5/4. If you haven't played in 5 since this section, it may feel a bit uncomfortable, so ease into it and count.

THURSDAY

The Samba ostinato is next. A faster tempo like this can be a real bear to sort out, so get the paradiddle locked in and then add the feet—or vice versa.

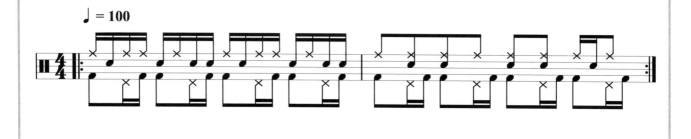

FRIDAY

Here, we jump back into bebop. Remember to use a light, swinging touch on the cymbal and to prevent the snare and bass drum from overpowering the ride and hi-hat.

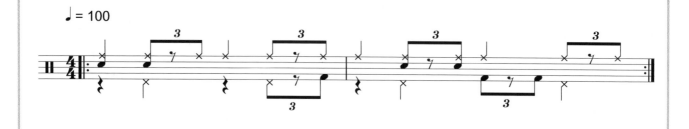

SATURDAY

Pattern 265 is a Baião groove. Since we haven't spent a whole lot of time on Baião patterns, you may not be able to push the tempo yet. No problem—just work the coordinations and gradually work on increasing the tempo.

SUNDAY

Pattern 266, a classic Afrobeat groove, rounds out Review 3. With this, you are working up a nice foundation in style comprehension. Congrats!

This week, we get into some tricky odd-time signatures with the eighth note as the bottom number. This generally means that tempos will be quicker because the eighth note now gets the beat. We introduce two new time signatures, 9/8 and 11/8, but you should recognize elements in them from previous odd meters. You can count odd meters in more than one way, and if you feel comfortable breaking them up—for example, "1, 2, 3, 1, 2, 3, 4" for counting in 7—then go ahead and do what works for you. There are no rules. That said, some songs may naturally accent some of the subdivisions in an odd measure, which can guide you to a counting system that works best for you. Listening to the audio examples will help, too, and I have marked the time signatures found in those songs to help you identify the meter. Some of the songs might be difficult to play, so start by just listening, then perhaps try to find some elements to play with.

MONDAY 267

5/8 is our first time signature and it can move by pretty fast. People often will count "1, 2, 1, 2, 3" or the reverse. You do what works best for you.

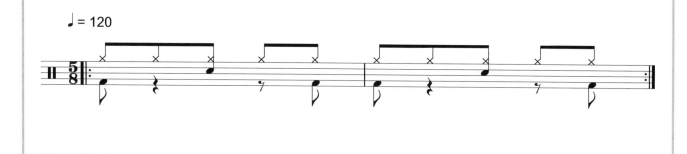

TUESDAY 268

Here is another pattern in 5/8. It almost has a trance-like feel to it, as it doesn't change much at all.

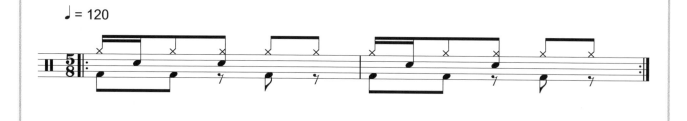

WEDNESDAY

Counting "1, 2, 3, 4, 1, 2, 3" is a very common approach to 7/8, but some count "1, 2, 1, 2, 1, 2, 3," as well. Alternatively, you can count right to 7 if you want to. The notes here are all familiar; it's the math of the notes that is the tricky part.

♩ = 120

THURSDAY

This groove has a familiar feel to it, as it has turned up in lots of progressive rock songs.

♩ = 120

FRIDAY

9/8 allows us to spread the groove out a bit more, giving us the opportunity to phrase the pattern many different ways within the measure.

♩ = 120

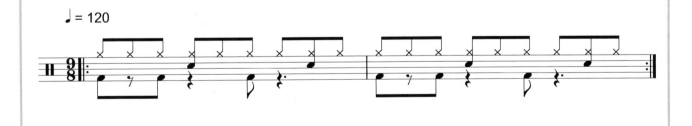

SATURDAY

Our last 9/8 groove gets a bit more complex, but once you cycle it a bit, you'll hear how it turns around and you'll be able to lock it in.

SUNDAY

11/8 is the final time signature in this section. This meter can be thought of as a bar of 6/8 and a bar of 5/8 or any other way you want to divide the notes. Again, a longer measure gives us new ways to build a groove and can be very exciting and challenging. Listen to the examples to hear some great ways to frame a measure.

SUGGESTED LISTENING AND PLAY-ALONGS:
- "Four Sticks" Led Zeppelin (5/8 and 6/8)
- "Subdivisions" Rush (7/8)
- "Seven Days" Sting (5/4)
- "Fool for You" The Impressions (9/8)
- "Frame by Frame" King Crimson (7/8 and 13/8)

NOTABLE DRUMMERS:
- Neil Peart
- Jack DeJohnette
- Tomas Haake
- Marco Minnemann
- Billy Cobham

WEEK 40: BEBOP 2

Bebop 2 focuses on breaking up the bass drum and snare via triplet figures, which can be challenging, as it pushes the independence of your limbs, including keeping your ride hand locked on the ride pattern. This week's patterns are common figures in bebop and are an introduction to the complex varieties that the great jazz drummers pioneered from the '40s through the '60s. A note about the listening section here is that a lot of bebop gets into very fast tempos and the explorations of the drummers get very complex. Don't be intimidated by all of this. Work on your control and relaxation when pushing for faster tempos. It may take some time beyond this book to get to those tempos together.

MONDAY   274

This first pattern features a straight triplet figure between your feet and snare hand as it alternates from bass drum to hi-hat for the first note of each triplet in measure 2. This works against the jazz ride pattern that you need to hold steady throughout.

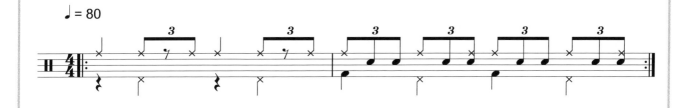

TUESDAY   275

Pattern 275 puts the emphasis on the bass drum playing the second and third note of the triplet on each beat (measure 2). You may feel off-balance when doing this. That isn't uncommon, as playing the triplet between your feet while the ride is holding steady can be tough due to the different sounds of the hi-hat and bass drum.

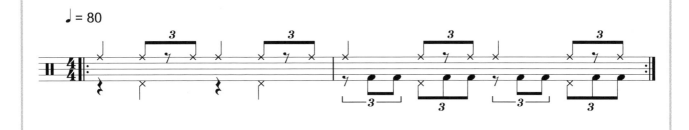

WEDNESDAY

This pattern breaks up the triplet further between the snare and bass drum from beat to beat. The hi-hat and ride are your anchors for this pattern, so keep them really consistent.

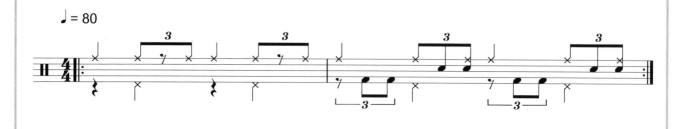

THURSDAY

The snare falls on the middle note of the triplet for each beat here, and the bass drum finishes the triplet on beats 1 and 3.

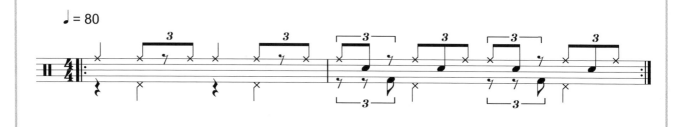

FRIDAY

Pattern 278 focuses on the snare, which plays the first two notes of the triplet for every beat—very common stuff in jazz and bebop. Make sure the second note of each beat is in the right spot and not too late.

Here, we take the same groupings of notes and alternate between the bass and snare on each beat. This could be performed many ways and on different parts of the triplet.

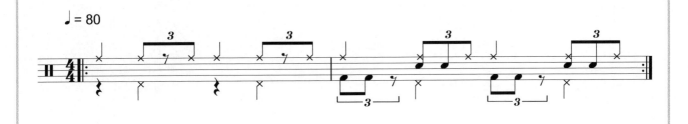

We lock down a two-measure phrase for the seventh pattern this week. You can mix and match any of the patterns from this section for longer phrases.

SUGGESTED LISTENING AND PLAY-ALONGS:
- "Cherokee" Clifford Brown and Max Roach
- "Solar" Bill Evans
- "I Want to Be Happy" Bud Powell
- "Boogie Stop Shuffle" Charles Mingus
- "Blue Serge" Kenny Clarke

NOTABLE DRUMMERS:
- Art Taylor
- Ben Riley
- Shelly Manne
- Louis Hayes
- Stan Levey

WEEK 41: MAMBO 2

Mambo 2 continues where we left off, the 2-3 rhumba clave, and then we move to new ride patterns and continue to alternate the claves. These subtle changes can be very difficult to deal with, so be patient. This is tough material, especially if you are new to it. When you're listening to the songs, try to find, count, and clap (or tap) the clave, as this will help you to understand how to phrase your parts on the kit.

MONDAY   281

Here is the 2-3 rhumba clave with accents now on beats 1 and 3 of every measure. You can go to the bell to accentuate the sound or just soften your notes on the ride. Try both for different textures.

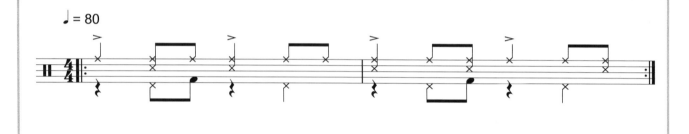

TUESDAY   282

This groove features a new ride pattern and the 3-2 son clave, with the accents now shifting to beats 2 and 4. We will be seeing accents regularly for the Mambo moving forward, so watch to see how they evolve.

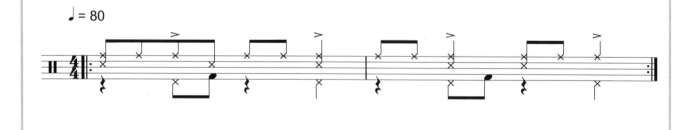

WEDNESDAY

283

This pattern features the 2-3 son clave and a new ride pattern. You can use the neck of the stick to accentuate the bell sound if you like.

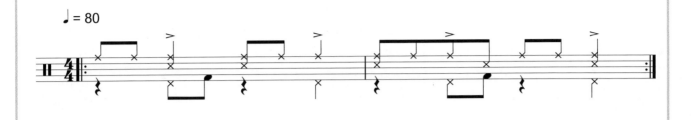

THURSDAY

284

The 3-2 rhumba clave and another new ride pattern are featured in Pattern 284. It doesn't seem like much, but often just a single-note shift can really change how you feel and play a pattern. So, it's important to make sure that you're changing up things when you intended to and not playing the pattern you did before, as it's a lot to keep track of.

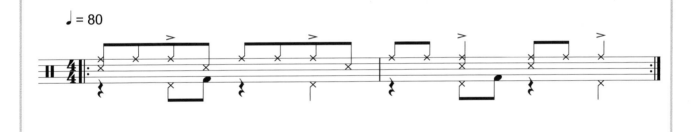

FRIDAY

285

We flip the hi-hat pattern from yesterday for this 2-3 rhumba clave while working the same accents. Make sure your bass drum isn't overpowering your cross stick.

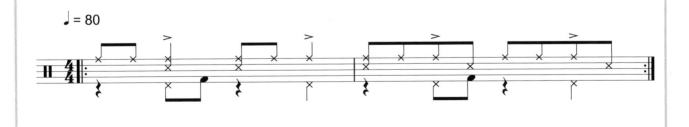

The cáscara rhythm on the ride and the 3-2 son clave is our next pattern—and it's a big one. The *cáscara rhythm* is often played on the shell of the floor tom, and I suggest that you work up the rhythm on that, as well. If you don't want to hit the shell of your floor tom, then you can use the rim. Just make sure to play all the accents.

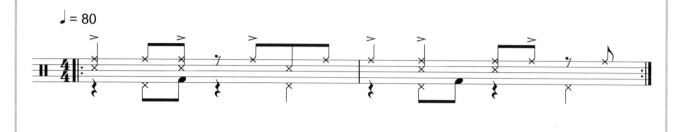

Here is the 2-3 son clave with the cáscara rhythm. The cáscara rhythm is very common in Mambo and many forms of Latin music. Ideally, you want to shift from cáscara to any one of the cymbal bell patterns or cowbell. If you can do that, then you'll have a basic handle on this approach, and it'll just be a matter of understanding song forms.

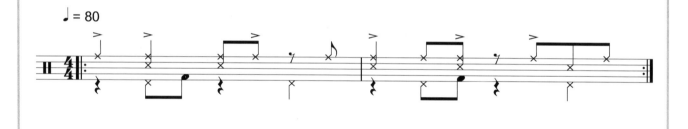

SUGGESTED LISTENING AND PLAY-ALONGS:
- "Mambo No. 5" Perez Prado
- "Mambo Gazón" Tito Puente
- "Azucar" Eddie Palmieri
- "Mambo Manila" Tito Rodriguez
- "La Dicha Mia" Celia Cruz

NOTABLE DRUMMERS:
- Alex Acuña
- Ignacio Berroa
- Guillermo Barreto
- Sheila E
- Giovanni Hidalgo

WEEK 42: METAL 3

The last week of metal patterns gets deeper into double bass work and the use of 32nd notes, as well as mixing triplets and 16th notes in different groupings. If you're performing these as single strokes, make sure that they're even and clean at slower tempos before trying faster patterns. Also, you can experiment with different stroke combinations, using doubles on one foot if you have the dexterity to do so. In other words, the patterns don't have to be played exclusively with single strokes.

MONDAY   288

The first pattern gets us into 32nd notes. Keep everything super clean and try to put as much space in between every note, giving each one its own clarity and space.

TUESDAY   289

We mix 16ths and 32nds here. It's important not to rush the faster notes. Go slow at first so you can hear the differences between the notes and then speed things up.

WEDNESDAY

We go back and forth between groups of four 32nds and four 16ths, which is a lot of notes to play. If you want to mix up the order of notes, you certainly can; otherwise, I recommend alternating single strokes all the way through at first.

THURSDAY

Pattern 291 switches up the placement of the 32nd notes, which may throw you off a bit. But if you don't rush it, you should be able to line things up nicely.

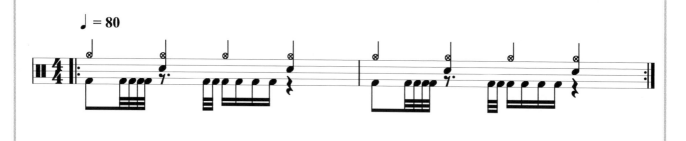

FRIDAY

Sixteenth-note triplets show up here. They should be a bit easier to play than the 32nds, although you might want to experiment with switching your lead foot.

SATURDAY

Mixing up 16th notes and triplets can be tricky because of the different subdivisions. This array of notes is very common, though, and once you get it down, you'll likely hear it in lots of music.

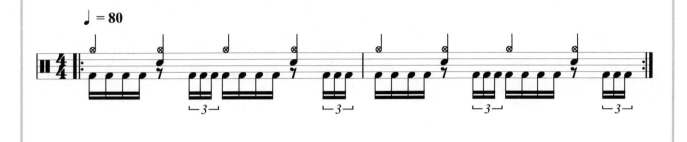

SUNDAY

Our last metal pattern is a hybrid of all the notes from this section. If the triplets throw you off, then go back and practice any of the patterns through the week and experiment with changing your lead foot.

SUGGESTED LISTENING AND PLAY-ALONGS:
- "Hot for Teacher" Van Halen
- "Shepherd of Fire" Avenged Sevenfold
- "Beneath" Meshuggah
- "Constant Motion" Dream Theater
- "Angel of Death" Slayer

NOTABLE DRUMMERS:
- Alex Van Halen
- Simon Phillips
- Virgil Donati
- Gene Hoglan
- Joey Jordison

WEEK 43: BEBOP 3

The third, and final, week of bebop takes us deeper into bass drum/snare drum interactions within triplets, but you can go much, much deeper into working on your independence within this style. The great pioneers of this style eventually pushed to four-limbed independence, which involves movement in each part of the kit in musical, highly dexterous ways. If you enjoy this study, I highly suggest reading any of the great jazz/bebop method books that are available, as well as spending time transcribing and/or listening to the extended works of the great jazz musicians listed at the end of this section.

MONDAY   295

The first pattern works the snare and bass drum across a two-measure phrase that utilizes some note combinations that you have seen previously.

TUESDAY   296

Pattern 296 features the bass drum in some new placements across the measure. This can be tricky, so you may need to break up the hands and feet and then assemble them later.

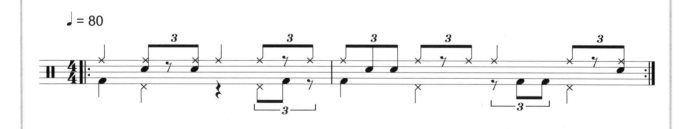

WEDNESDAY

Here, we gradually add more notes to the pattern. This is a good exercise for building your coordinations and you can pull elements from it to use in musical situations.

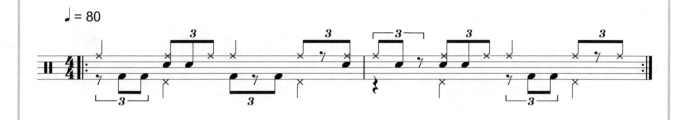

THURSDAY

Pattern 298 adds more bass drum notes to the front end of measure 2. Watch your ride cymbal pattern to make sure it doesn't break from the sequence.

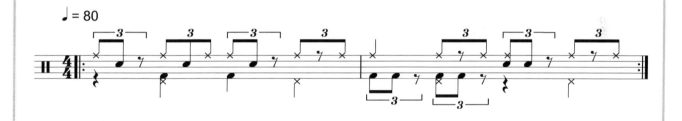

FRIDAY

It may help to think of the hi-hat as the focal point of each measure and, between that and the ride cymbal, you can place notes around them as long as those two elements remain static. As the note content increases, however, you may need to try different approaches to sorting the patterns.

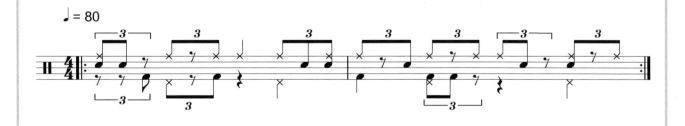

SATURDAY

Pattern 300 features some single bass and snare notes in the middle of the triplet ride pattern, which can be tricky, so try to adhere to the flow and spacing of the triplet.

SUNDAY

Again, snare and bass drum notes within the triplets work against the ride pattern, which may take a bit to line up. This type of phrasing is commonly used in jazz and bebop.

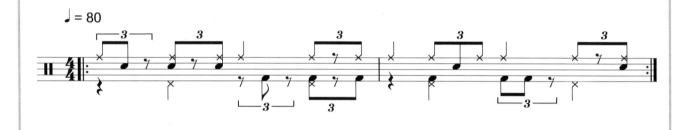

SUGGESTED LISTENING AND PLAY-ALONGS:
- "Cheese Cake" Dexter Gordon
- "Matrix" Chick Corea
- "Moritat" Sonny Rollins
- "My Jelly Roll Soul" Charles Mingus
- "Song for My Father" Horace Silver

NOTABLE DRUMMERS:
- Brian Blade
- Alan Dawson
- Paul Motian
- Carl Allen
- Jeff Watts

WEEK 44: BEATS USING TOMS

We interrupt our work on Latin and jazz grooves to jump into some rock-oriented patterns that use toms and floor toms as integral parts to the groove. These patterns can be played many different ways and, like with the rest of the book, the sticking choices are yours. This approach to phrasing a groove on the toms and floor toms can be applied to all styles of music and dates way back to the origins of the drum set. Incidentally, much Latin music can be played this way to replicate the sounds that hand percussionists make when they play with a group that has no drum set and when they are phrasing different melodic ideas.

MONDAY   302

Pattern 302 is a classic "surf beat" that is common in '60s-style music and is a good workout for your floor-tom hand.

TUESDAY   303

Here, we run 16th notes between the floor tom and bass drum, which approximates a double-bass groove. If you keep the notes balanced and even, the pattern will come across great.

WEDNESDAY

Pattern 304 falls into the shuffle category and is used a lot in rock grooves. Make sure the notes have a strong swing and drive along with the bass drum.

THURSDAY

This is a Latin-style pattern that is frequently used in rock grooves. Keep the ride steady and move the opposite hand from the snare to the rack tom and floor tom.

FRIDAY

Pattern 306 can be broken up between your hands or performed with one hand on the tom and floor tom. Do it the way you feel most comfortable but keep the hi-hat steady, with your foot doing eighth notes.

SATURDAY

The paradiddle arrives as the foundation of this groove and is the easiest way to play this pattern steadily. Changing up the sticking might make it harder to play.

♩ = 85

SUNDAY

You can use whichever sticking combination you prefer for this 6/8 groove. Just make it work for you and your coordination.

♩ = 80

SUGGESTED LISTENING AND PLAY-ALONGS:
- "Sing, Sing, Sing" Benny Goodman Orchestra
- "Lateralus" Tool
- "Topsy Parts 1 and 2" Cozy Cole
- "Grace" Jeff Buckley
- "Bo Diddley" Bo Diddley

NOTABLE DRUMMERS:
- Jimmy Chamberlin
- Max Roach
- Phil Collins
- Art Blakey
- Terry Bozzio

WEEK 45: ODD-TIME JAZZ

Odd meters in jazz are relatively uncommon but they are certainly something that can be—and have been—explored at length. This week features several examples of jazz-style grooves in odd meters. As you put together the coordinations, count your way through the patterns to ensure your accuracy.

MONDAY 309

3/4 time is first up this week and there are many ways to phrase it. Lock down the ride pattern first and then add the other notes.

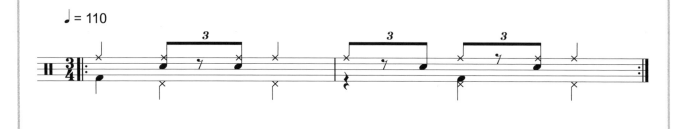

TUESDAY 310

Pattern 310 is also in 3/4 and it brings in some of the coordinations that you have seen in the bebop material.

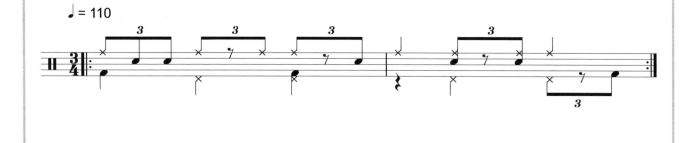

WEDNESDAY

Here, we move into 5/4 time, which can swing quite nicely. Watch the hi-hat and bass drum notes, as they anchor the pattern.

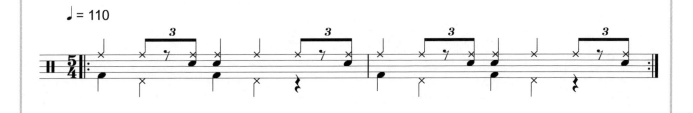

THURSDAY

6/8 is the same sort of flow as 3/4 but sometimes it swings a bit easier. The bass lands on beat 1 and the hi-hat on beat 4, which can make this groove swing.

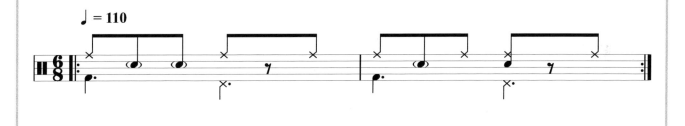

FRIDAY

7/4 swings in a cool way and is an interesting way to approach playing jazz. If it makes things easier, you can count 7/4 as a bar of 4 and a bar of 3 combined

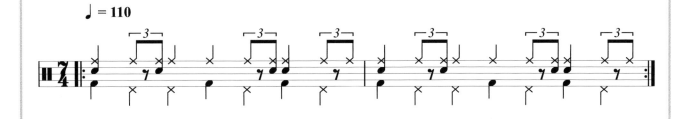

SATURDAY

7/8 offers a unique way to approach a swing feel and can be approached many ways. For example, this pattern can be phrased with just the snare and ride first, adding the feet later.

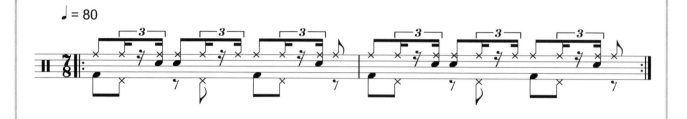

SUNDAY

This last pattern is a measure of 3/4 and 5/4 side by side. Work each measure up first and then bring them together or try the ride back to back and then add the other elements.

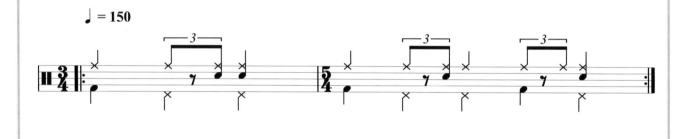

SUGGESTED LISTENING AND PLAY-ALONGS:
- "My Favorite Things" John Coltrane (3/4)
- "Take Five" Dave Brubeck (5/4)
- "Flood" Snarky Puppy (7/4)
- "Pussy Wiggle Stomp" Don Ellis (7/8)
- "Footloose and Fancy Free" Bill Bruford's Earthworks (5/4, 7/4, and 3/4)

NOTABLE DRUMMERS:
- Ralph Humphrey
- Chester Thompson
- Elvin Jones
- Vinnie Colaiuta
- Keith Carlock

WEEK 46: BAIÃO OSTINATOS

This last section of ostinatos is the toughest one in this book, as we use the Baião foot pattern as the foundation of this work. You probably already found some frustration with the first week of Baião, so you know what this is about. The good news is that a lot of the hand patterns are derivatives of other ostinatos you've learned. Going through this week of patterns, though, will push your coordination ahead considerably and prep you for the second week of Baião, which is coming up soon.

MONDAY   316

Sixteenth notes on the snare drum is the first pattern. Of course, like always, you can try different sticking ideas and then move your hands about the kit.

TUESDAY   317

Here, we look at two notes per surface (bar 2), which, in this case, is played either RRLL or LLRR.

WEDNESDAY

Here, the pattern goes in the other direction, starting on the snare and moving to the ride. After you get this down, try moving the ride cymbal hand to another sound source and see how that works with the ostinato.

THURSDAY

Here, we move the doubles to the inside and outside portions of the pattern, which you have seen before. Pay attention to how it lines up with the bass drum notes.

FRIDAY

Pattern 320 is a reversal of the last pattern. Sometimes just a change in direction can open up different doors in you coordination. Always count so you can be sure of your accuracy.

SATURDAY

Here, the paradiddle pops back again and can be a good litmus test for new coordination scenarios that you face.

♩ = 80

SUNDAY

This last ostinato is a hybrid of the ideas that you worked on in this section. If you feel good about this, or any of the patterns, you can add different elements to them. For example, you can accent or ghost certain notes, you can move to different surfaces for different sounds, and/or you can remove notes to break up the pattern. Of course, you can also devise your own ostinato figures to play over. Experiment! This material is only a starting point—there is much, much more you can strive for.

♩ = 80

SUGGESTED LISTENING AND PLAY-ALONGS:
- "Baião a Tempo" Luciana Souza
- "Wake Up Song" Airto Moreira
- "Cachaca (Baião)" Patrick Moraz
- "Carnival Baião" Watazu
- "Baião" João Paulo Amaral

NOTABLE DRUMMERS:
- Gregg Bissonette
- Joey Heredia
- Don Alias
- Dafnis Prieto
- Steve Berrios

WEEK 47: SONGO

Songo is a Cuban form of music and is one of the few Latin styles that actually originated on the drum set, not percussion. The great drummer Changuito (José Luis Quintana) is the man credited with creating the patterns and he's done videos and recorded much music demonstrating this groove. Songo can be taken in many directions but has been applied to funk and Latin-funk music in particular.

MONDAY
323

As we get into some of the more difficult material in this book, be patient with the process. Songo may be tough at first and extend the time it takes you to get through the patterns, but if you apply the techniques you've been honing throughout the book, you will have breakthroughs.

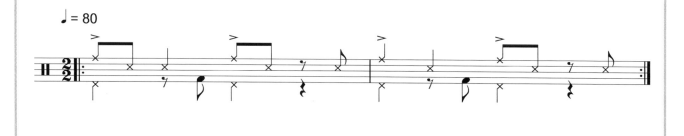

TUESDAY
324

This week's second groove is similar to the first but contains more bass drum notes. If your hands are locked in from the previous pattern, break the bass drum into one-measure sections, joining the hands and feet when ready.

WEDNESDAY

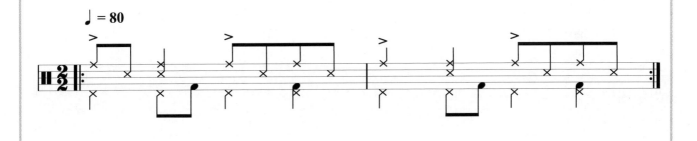

Pattern 325 changes the ride to quarter notes but otherwise is just like Pattern 323.

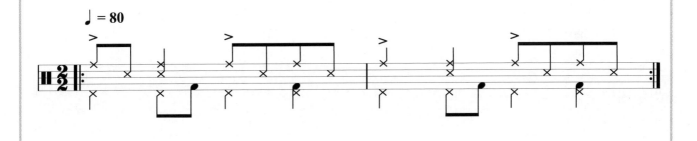

THURSDAY

Here, we change the ride and cross-stick patterns a bit. In this case, I suggest working the hands first, then the feet.

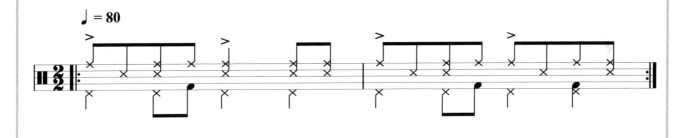

FRIDAY

The cross stick and bass drum patterns change in this example. Like Pattern 326, it makes sense to break this groove up into sections, as it might be tough to assemble all at once.

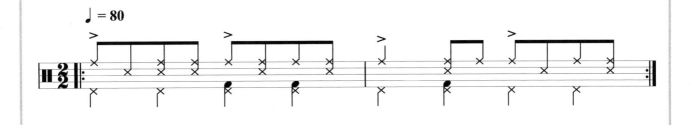

SATURDAY

Pattern 328 changes the ride but also uses familiar notes around it. In this case, the ride should be addressed first, adding parts when you get it locked down.

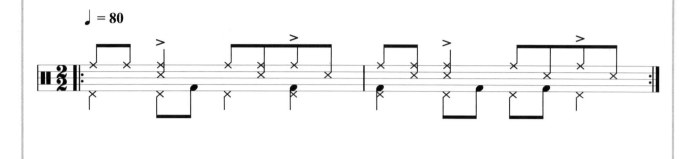

SUNDAY

Our last Songo groove applies the cáscara rhythm to the cross stick, which makes for a busier pattern. If you struggle with this, review the cáscara from Mambo 2 (Week 41). Here, you can substitute the snare for the cross stick but you should listen to the audio examples, as the snare notes are often phrased as ghost notes, which takes some attention to detail.

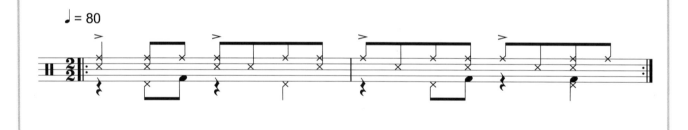

SUGGESTED LISTENING AND PLAY-ALONGS:
- "Y Ya Tu Campana No Suena" Los Van Van
- "Caribe" Michel Camilo
- "Con el Bate de Aluminio" Los Van Van
- "La Bruja" NG La Banda
- "El coleccionista" David Calzado & La Charanga Habanera

NOTABLE DRUMMERS:
- Changuito (Jose Luis Quintana)
- David Garibaldi
- Calixto Oviedo
- Yoel Páez
- Hector Randy Olmo

WEEK 48: 6/8 NANIGO

Week 48 brings us to 6/8 Nanigo rhythms. These are also Afro-Cuban and can really add a lot of spice to the drum set. The rhythms, like most Afro-Cuban styles, originated on percussion, but the Nanigo has a bit more of an African feel to it. We will explore this exciting style by shifting back to the cross stick and moving to the toms and floor tom. These patterns can be phrased many ways and deeper study will show the numerous approaches to this highly complex style.

MONDAY 330

Pattern 330 is the classic groove in this style. Work up your hands first, playing the accents on the bell of the cymbal, then align them with the feet.

TUESDAY 331

Pattern 331 changes the floor tom a bit and there is an additional bass drum note. Be sure your accents are locked in.

WEDNESDAY

Pattern 332 contains some changes in the bass drum and eliminates a tom hit.

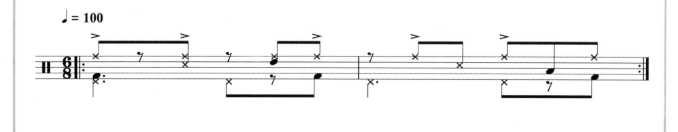

THURSDAY

There is a change to the cross stick in this groove, which may take you a bit to work up. Hands first, then sort the feet.

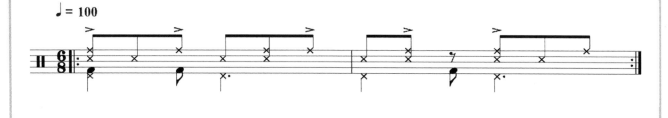

FRIDAY

In Pattern 334, the cross-stick is placed in some spots that you may not be used to. This can make the feel come across differently, so check to make sure your ride pattern is locked in because the whole groove, like all of the others, revolves around its consistency.

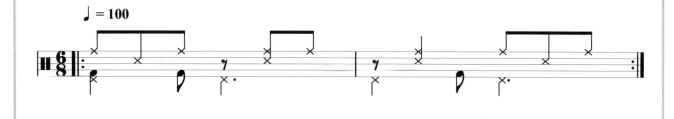

SATURDAY

We slide back to the snare for this groove, which gives it a backbeat feel. Make sure that you bring out the accent at the top of the second measure, as it's important to the feel of this pattern.

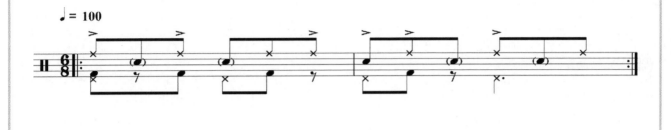

SUNDAY

This week's final pattern is a bit sparser and keeps the snare engaged. The space in the groove will help you to hear this style in a different light.

SUGGESTED LISTENING AND PLAY-ALONGS:
- "A Love Supreme" John Coltrane
- "Panamericana Suite" Paquito D'Rivera
- "Afro Blue" Poncho Sanchez
- "Villa Hidalgo" Giovanni Hidalgo
- "Gandinga, mondongo sandunga" Afro-Cuban All Stars

NOTABLE DRUMMERS:
- Dennis Chambers
- Rodney Holmes
- Antonio Sanchez
- Walfredo Reyes Jr.
- Giovanni Hidalgo

WEEK 49: BAIÃO 2

The last week of Baião brings back some familiar Brazilian rhythms. If you find yourself breezing through the material this week, try orchestrating your snare hand around the toms and floor. Also try some buzzes and rimshots in place of the snare notes.

MONDAY

337

We add a new ride pattern this week but it's one you encountered in the Samba and other styles. That said, the pattern may take a bit of practice before you're able to bring it into this groove.

♩ = 80

TUESDAY

338

Pattern 338 features more note combinations on the snare. You can play these as cross sticks, as well.

♩ = 80

WEDNESDAY

In this pattern, the snare continues to get more active. You can change the sound of the groove by adding some accents and playing some of the notes very softly.

THURSDAY

Keep in mind the role of the bass drum here and make sure it doesn't overpower the rest of the kit. If you're playing it too loud, then I suggest backing up to Baião 1 (Week 33) and practicing a pattern that is easier for you while focusing on playing the bass drum softer. Then apply that approach to this section.

FRIDAY

Nothing too different here; just the snare dropped in some different spots.

SATURDAY

As you near the end of this section, take the time to start moving your snare hand to the toms and also try some rimshots and soft buzzes on the snare.

SUNDAY

Pattern 343 has similarities to the Partido Alto, which we saw in Bossa Nova 2 (Week 10). You can apply to this groove different combinations of notes from different sections and you can pull patterns from other books to work your independence.

SUGGESTED LISTENING AND PLAY-ALONGS:
- "Três E Trezentos" Luiz Gonzaga
- "Baião Destemperado" Barbatuques
- "Baião De Quatro Toques" Andrea Motis
- "Baião" Abacaxi
- "Baião em Howth" Igor Brasil

NOTABLE DRUMMERS:
- Guegué Medeiros
- Airto Moreira
- Wilson das Neves
- Michael Shrieve

WEEK 50: WEST AFRICAN

Like most Latin styles, West African drum-set styles are derived from percussion parts. The patterns included here are all rooted in either 6/8 or 12/8 meter but there are others that are in 4/4. Being that we have spent the majority of this book in straight time signatures, I wanted to focus a bit of time on 6/8 and 12/8 to illustrate some of the different ways you can approach them. Since they're compound time signatures, they can be felt and phrased in more ways than one.

MONDAY 344

Our first pattern is in 6/8. You will hear similarities to the Nanigo but there are differences, as well. The ride pattern here is less complex but there is more happening with the bass drum. You may need to start with just the bass drum, hi-hat, and ride, then add the cross stick.

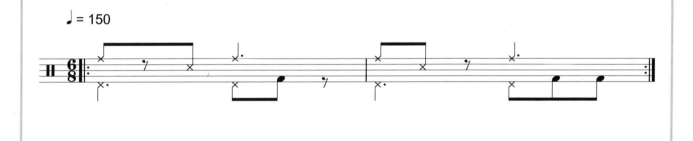

TUESDAY 345

Here's a sparse pattern. It's similar to the previous one but with fewer bass drum notes and different emphasis on the ride.

WEDNESDAY

Now we shift to 12/8 for a few grooves. We can really imply different feels within the 12/8 pulse. Once you lock down the repetitive ostinato pattern in the feet, you can address the hands. Although the hands play a lot of notes, measures 1 and 2 are identical.

♩ = 150

THURSDAY

Notice how the groove almost takes on a different feel by placing the cross stick in different spots in the measure. Once you get this pattern down, try to play it back to back with the previous groove. Even though you're playing the same bass and hi-hat notes, they will feel very different because the ride pattern has shifted.

♩ = 150

FRIDAY

Pattern 348 shifts the ride, leaving a space on beat 1. What's interesting about this feel is that you can move just one note across the measure and the groove has a fresh new sound, even though you are playing the same pattern.

♩ = 150

SATURDAY

Pattern 349 is entirely different and a great example of another way to approach this style of drumming and the flexibility of 12/8 time. We lay the bass drum in what almost feels like the backbeat of the groove, making the pattern feel inverted.

SUNDAY

In this pattern, notice how the bass drum is in 3/8 and the hi-hat is in 4/8. 12/8 can be looked at as four measures of 3/8 or three measures of 4/8—it's malleable and is determined by the way you present the feel. This is an example of both being implied. Play the feet by themselves first to hear how they interact, then add your hands.

SUGGESTED LISTENING AND PLAY-ALONGS:
- "Haina" Art Blakey
- "Makondi" Ed Blackwell and Don Cherry
- "Menu Di Ye Jewe" Babatunde Olatunji
- "Senegal" Mokhtar Samba
- "In Your Eyes" Peter Gabriel

NOTABLE DRUMMERS:
- Manu Katché
- Ed Blackwell
- Art Blakey
- Babatunde Olatunji
- Mokhtar Samba

WEEK 51: MOZAMBIQUE

The final week of new material is a quick venture into the Mozambique style. This is a Cuban style that has some interesting variations and also some similarities to other Afro-Cuban styles that you may recall.

MONDAY 351

Pay close attention to the accents in this section, as they add a lot to the feel. You may need to work those up first.

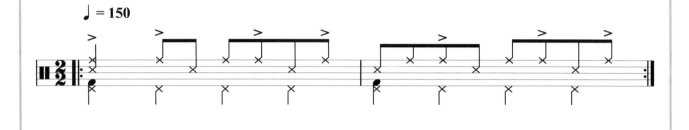

TUESDAY 352

Pattern 352 adds some more bass drum content but the cross stick and accented ride stays locked in.

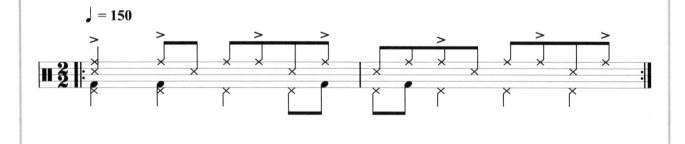

WEDNESDAY

Here, we change the ride pattern and accents but return to the bass/hi-hat figure we saw in the Mambo.

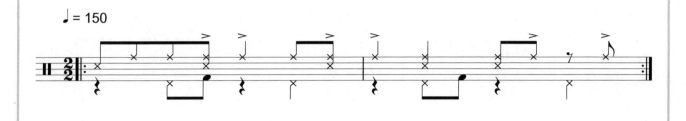

THURSDAY

Pattern 354 brings back the cáscara rhythm on the ride and also integrates the toms into the pattern. Meanwhile, the bass drum lands on the "one."

FRIDAY

Pattern 355 is the same as Thursday's groove but now we add some new notes to the bass drum.

SATURDAY

Pattern 356 alters the bass drum to mix up the groove a bit while keeping the hands locked on the same pattern.

SUNDAY

Pattern 357 is deceptive in that the additional bass drum notes create a shift in the way the groove flows. While familiarity in this and all Latin styles will help you adjust to these different approaches to phrasing a groove, lots of listening and research will help you as much as working up the patterns.

SUGGESTED LISTENING AND PLAY-ALONGS:
- "Late in the Evening" Paul Simon
- "Mi Mambo Conga" Eddie Palmieri
- "Mozambique International" Pello El Afrokán
- "María Caracoles" Afro-Cuban All Stars
- "Speak Low" McCoy Tyner

NOTABLE DRUMMERS:
- Elvin Jones
- Manny Oquendo
- Pedro Izquierdo
- Bobby Sanabria
- Pete Escovedo

This last review section covers a lot of ground stylistically and is the toughest to work up. As before, if you skipped the metal section, then substitute from any week that you enjoyed or feel you need to work on.

MONDAY   358

Here's a two-measure bebop phrase. Mind the dynamics on the bass drum and snare and push the tempo when you're ready.

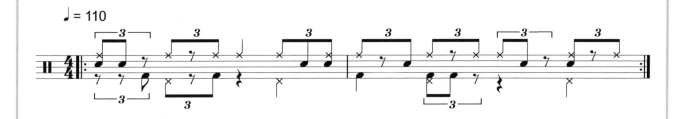

TUESDAY   359

Mambo comes next. Note the cáscara rhythm on the ride and the accents.

Pattern 360 hits the metal material and features some intricate double bass using 16th notes and 16th-note triplets.

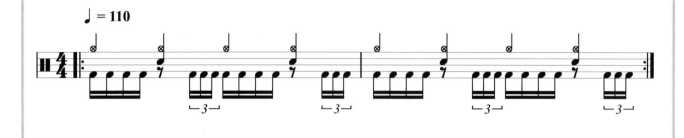

This Baião ostinato exercise uses the paradiddle (again!) against the repeating foot patterns.

Pattern 362 reviews 6/8 time and the Nanigo. The accents in this pattern make the groove really flow, so pay attention to those.

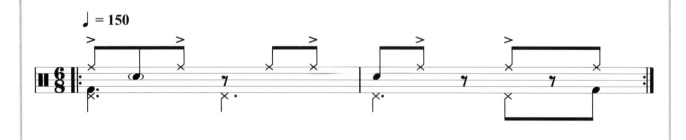

SATURDAY

7/4 is the time signature for this odd-time jazz groove, which can be counted "1, 2, 3, 1, 2, 3, 4" to help you along.

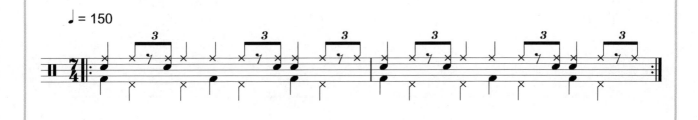

SUNDAY

This Mozambique pattern features a lot of activity in the cross stick, so go slow to lock it in and then speed it up when you're ready.

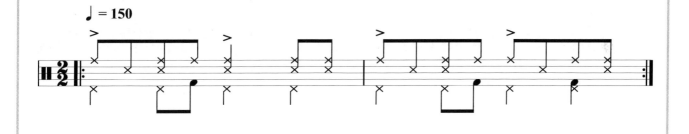

DAY 365

This bonus review pattern is an 11/8 groove from the Odd-Time Rock 2 section (Week 39). You can count this "1, 2, 3, 4, 5, 6, 1, 2, 3, 4, 5" to get the notes in the right spots.

FINAL THOUGHTS

Congratulations on making it through this book! I hope that by working through this material, you have been able to add new styles to your repertoire and have been introduced to some wonderful new music along the way! As you may have learned, there is a lot to discover on the drum set, and when you dig into different styles, your potential for development increases dramatically. If your mind is open and you become a student of music and its history, you will set yourself upon a path of endless discovery. I encourage you to go deeper into the styles that appeal to you via extended listening and books dedicated to the individual styles. Dig deep and enjoy digging deep into the details.

A question often asked is, "Where will I use this material?" That is a question that only you can answer. But remember: creative application should not be forced or expected. How and when you use this knowledge should not be the concern; on the contrary, if you focus on the quest, your development, and studying the music, over time you will work the material into your music world in a natural, logical way.

If you have any questions or comments, feel free to reach out to me via my website, *daveschoepke.com*. I would love to help you in any way I can.

ABOUT THE AUTHOR

Dave Schoepke hails from the Greater Milwaukee area. He has been a professional recording and touring musician for three decades, including treks across North America and Europe. His credits include Jethro Tull guitarist Martin Barre and songsmith Willy Porter. He has been a creative force in Willy's band since 2002.

An active session musician with appearances on over 50 albums, Dave does remote recording from his home studio for artists worldwide. He appears on the recordings of such diverse artists as Bryan Lee, Darrell Scott, Natalia Zukerman, Raining Jane, Billy Flynn, Doug Woolverton, Victor DeLorenzo, Michael Bettine, Russ Johnson, Todd Sickafoose, Brian Ritchie, Chuck Garrick, Allison Miller, Ray Bonneville, Paul Cebar, and Alan Thomson. Dave also appears on over a dozen instructional CDs for Hal Leonard, covering many genres.

His solo drums project has produced three all-drums albums and garnered acclaimed reviews from *Modern Drummer*, *Recording Magazine*, and numerous online music critics around the world. The 400th issue of *Recording Magazine* includes a multi-page feature on Dave's process of writing and recording his album *Drums on Low*.

Dave has been teaching drums for over 30 years and has done numerous clinics and educational-based symposiums with legendary artists Jeff Coffin, Ed Thigpen, Paul Wertico, Dom Famularo, Gregg Bissonette, and Carmine Appice. He maintains a busy schedule of teaching, touring, clinics, and sessions and is always striving to evolve in every facet of his music-making. For lesson inquiries or questions, Dave can be reached via his website, *daveschoepke.com.*

Made in the USA
Las Vegas, NV
29 July 2023

75402090R00090